Story Telling Twelve

STORY TELLING TWELVE

Sept 2018

STORY TELLING TWELVE

A DIFFERENT SLANT ON LIFE

ISBN 978 1 9164697 0 9

Published by

Percychatteybooks Publisher

Story Telling Twelve

Featuring Famous Names of the Past

This month we look at

Lawrence of Arabia and Cleopatra.

As told by Richard Seal

Also

Part Three Of Terry Tumblers Novel

The Rough and Tumbles of Early Life

STORY TELLING TWELVE

Percychatteybooks is self-regulating to the contents and reserves the right to alter, change or edit articles and is not responsible for any advice given or knowledge that is imparted and recommendation, guidance or information should be checked on independently before acting on it.

All the individual works in Story Telling are published with full authority of the originator. *If the reader needs further information concerning one of our 'Story Tellers' then please send an email to* percybooks@outlook.com *we will pass your request on to them*

As always my gratitude to my lovely wife Jean, friend and soul mate, who has helped with the editing and all rewrites, also listening to all my ramblings whilst putting these articles together.

My appreciation to the following

Derek Cook for the cover

Richard Seal

Janette Menday

Trudie Oakley

Terry Tumbler

Carole Llewellyn

Lin Penhaul

Christopher Wyatt

Frank Schaeffer

Sarah Dawkins

Ellie Jenkins

Content

My name is Meg, and as in the past I will be your host throughout this creation. But First let me explain the following as it is very important:

The contents and the opinions shown or written here are not necessarily the views of 'Story Telling' or its publisher and are published as articles of interest and amusement only and no offence of any kind religious, racial or political is intended to any person or group of people.

I would also like to add on behalf of Story Telling, in a world where there is so much fake and dishonest stories being bandied around, we cannot guarantee any item printed here as being accurate or correct and should be checked on before acting on them.

We will start with this item from around seventy years ago

Tips to look after your husband

(Extract from 1950 Home Economics Book)

Have dinner ready
Plan ahead, even the night before, to have a delicious meal on time. This is a way of letting him know that you have been thinking about him and are concerned about his needs. Most men are hungry when they come home and the prospects of a good meal are part of the warm welcome needed.

Prepare yourself
Take 15 minutes to rest so you will be refreshed when he arrives. Touch up your make-up, put a ribbon in your hair and be fresh looking. He has just been with a lot of work weary people. Be a little gay and a little more interesting. His boring day may need a lift.

Clear away the clutter
Make one last trip through the main part of the house just before your husband arrives, gathering up school books, toys, paper etc. Then run a dust cloth over the tables. Your husband will feel he has reached a haven of rest and order, and it will give you a lift too.

Prepare the children
Take a few minutes to wash the children's hands and faces (if they are small), comb their hair, and if necessary, change their clothes. They are little treasures and he would like to see them playing the part.

Minimise all noise
At the time of his arrival, eliminate all noise of washer, drier dishwasher or vacuum. Try to encourage the children to be quiet. Be happy to see him. Greet him with a warm smile and be glad to see him.

Some don'ts
Don't greet him with problems or complaints. Don't complain if he's late for dinner. Count this as minor compared with what he might have gone through that day.

Make him comfortable
Have him lean back in a comfortable chair or suggest he lie down in the bedroom. Have a cool or warm drink ready for him. Arrange his pillow and offer to take off his shoes. Speak in a low, soft, soothing and pleasant voice. Allow him to relax - unwind.

Is Sex Work or Pleasure

An RAF Group Captain was about to start the morning briefing to his staff ....

Whilst waiting for the coffee machine to finish its brewing, the Group Captain decided to pose a question to all assembled. He explained that his wife had been a bit frisky the night before and he failed to get his usual amount of sound sleep.

He posed the question of just how much of sex was "work" and how much of it was "pleasure"

A Wing Commander chimed in with 75-25% in favour of work. A Squadron Leader said it was 50-50%.
A Flight Lieutenant responded with 25-75% in favour of pleasure, depending upon his state of inebriation at the time.

There being no consensus, the Group Captain turned to the young Corporal who was in charge of making the coffee. What the Group Captain wondered was his opinion?

Without any hesitation, the young Corporal responded, "Sir, it has to be 100% pleasure."

> The Group Captain was surprised and, as you might guess, asked "And, why exactly would that be the case?"

The young Corporal replied, "Well, sir, if there was any work involved, the officers would have me doing it for them."

The room fell silent.

****

The Architectural Designer

When designing new houses it is important to carry out serious investigative work before starting otherwise some hidden problem will rear up and then bring the whole project to an end or alternately a costly renovation to cure the problem.

It was on such on occasion when we were called to a house in West Bristol. The property had been built before the Second World War; it was a large detached residence in a street of similar design. The owners wanted to convert the very large cellar to a snooker and games room.

The thoroughfare leading to the home was built on the side of a steep hill. The houses on one side backed onto the abrupt rise behind them. The ones opposite were similar in that they were two storeys high and although the front door, hall and living area were at street level, immediately below

them there was a steep void and the dwelling was built on stilts.

When the original design was carried out they, the designers, and the builders who followed never took in consideration that there was a water course flowing at right angles to the house, this apparently was buried below the houses opposite and no doubt had been sunk below the roadway.

On inspection I discovered that over the years various attempts had been made to change the direction of the water flow. One attempt had been to try and divert it to the side of the building, by installing a long deep French type drain, going across the front of the house between it and the road, had been constructed to achieve this. Without success!

In the basement the water was seeping in through the wall large amounts and bi-passing the plastic and cement structure of the drain, by going below it. To try and stop this, again without achieving any result a thick eighteen inch concrete wall had been constructed against the original wall in the cellar. No doubt it had solved the problem when it was built. However, over time, the water was going to have its way and had penetrated it and leaked into the cellar.

The basement was unusable because of the moisture and damp (also a few mushrooms), but in other ways it was ideal for the client's needs of turning it into a games room. I set about finding a way of curing what was a serious moist problem as the water was soaking into the dirt of the unmade floor and I could see over time this could possibly make the house unstable.

First things first, a total survey was carried out to understand not only the structure of the house but also where the utilities were, floor levels also room sizes, construction and support points and whatever was there needed to be included within the dimensions.

Because the ground sloped away steeply - where the water was entering the property the head height was at about nine feet. At the rear of the house overlooking a level manicured garden it was nearly double that. So it was obvious if we were going to put a snooker table in there, which the client had told me he desired, then the floor would have to be level.

With the survey out of the way I was sitting at the drawing board and studying the 'section diagram' of the assessment and puzzling the problem, when suddenly it became very obvious. (A section drawing is a slice of the project similar to what you see when you cut a slice of cake). It was obvious stop trying to divert the water and let it have its own way by opening up a channel in the concrete wall and then lay twelve inch plastic piping in the ground, with a level floor over, and direct the water through it and out of the rear of the house.

To the front of the proposed cellar where the water entered I designed an opening in the old concrete wall specifying a plastic insert to stop the water seeping into the concrete. This was directed down the wall into pipe work laid in the floor.

To hide all this engineering work I created a tiled Toilet Room in stud walls with facilities in them to inspect the new water channel which was in the constructed behind it, also a further inspection chamber in the floor where the pipe work running to the rear began. I also included a waste channel for the W.C which went to the rear and joined the original sewage system which had been laid in the rear garden.

The rest of the floor area was constructed on two levels and as there was masses of room there was plenty of space for the snooker table and other facilities' including a bar area overlooking the rear with views across the landscape.

Although not in my design, the owner successfully ran the pipe work carrying the water buried it in the garden and directed it to a pond in which he reared fish.

****

Observations on Growing Older:

Going out is good. Coming home is better!

Saturday Morning Picture Show

By Richard Seal

As a child of the nineteen seventies, Dan had loved Saturday morning movie magic at his local cinema: Having a great time larking around in the dark with his school friends, barely watching the screen, in the comforting sugar-warmth of popcorn and candy fug. The cartoon and supporting feature often passed him by before everyone settled down (to a degree) to watch the main feature. He wondered why there were so many Elvis films and all the westerns seemed to be much the same, usually starring John Wayne.

Returning to this precious place many times in his twenties, Dan loved to get lost in the big screen, enveloped by shared trance, enhanced by luxuriating in soft-focus nostalgia. He was overjoyed to find that most of the cramped and tatty fixtures and fittings remained, although it was not quite the same somehow without the aged usherette he remembered from his childhood - he had bought so many ice creams from her tray, before joining his mates in throwing the wrappers through the projector beam.

By his thirties, Dan was only able to visit the cinema occasionally, but every time was a special occasion. He now preferred a quiet corner at the back of the room which seemed to be reserved just for him. Diet suspended for a couple of hours, he relished the prospect of tackling his large bag of chocolate peanuts and raisins. Dan did not mind what film he was watching, he was just glad to be there, to feel that familiar shivery thrill as he hugged himself and relaxed sitting beside the velvet curtain, head resting against his own personal purple pillar.

Having spent much of his youth enamoured of his beloved cinema, Dan went on to spend his forties fighting to preserve and protect its Art Deco facade; it was a long, hard road - many meetings and letters were required before the necessary permissions were secured and the building could finally be saved. A vast' state-of-the-art shopping mall now stands on the site ... The cinema burned to the ground on the eve of Dan's fiftieth birthday - the wiring, old and faulty, took the blame.

****

Observations on Growing Older: You read 100 pages into a book before you realize you've read it.

****

The 5 pounds you wanted to lose is now 15 and you have a better chance of losing your keys than the 15 pounds.

John is my heart

By Frank Schaeffer of the Washington Post.

This is a well-written article about a father who put several of his kids through expensive colleges but one son wanted to be a Marine. Interesting observation by this dad - an interesting commentary that says a lot about our society

"Before my son became a Marine, I never thought much about who was defending me. Now when I read of the war on terrorism or the coming conflict in Iraq, it cuts to my heart. When I see a picture of a member of our military who has been killed, I read his or her name very carefully. Sometimes I cry.

In 1999, when the barrel-chested Marine recruiter showed up in dress blues and bedazzled my son John, I did not stand in the way. John was headstrong, and he seemed to understand these stern, clean men with straight backs and flawless uniforms. I did not. I live in the Volvo-driving, higher education-worshiping North Shore of Boston . I write novels for a living. I have never served in the military.

It had been hard enough sending my two older children off to Georgetown and New York University. John's enlisting was unexpected, so deeply unsettling. I did not relish the prospect of answering the question, "So where is John going to college?" from the parents who were itching to tell me all about how their son or daughter was going to Harvard. At the private high school John attended, no other students were going into the military.

"But aren't the Marines terribly Southern?" (Says a lot about open-mindedness in the Northeast) asked one perplexed mother while standing next to me at the brunch following graduation. "What a waste, he was such a good student," said another parent. One parent (a professor at a nearby and rather famous university) spoke up at a school meeting and suggested that the school should, "carefully evaluate what went wrong."

When John graduated from three months of boot camp on Parris Island, 3000 parents and friends were on the parade deck stands. We parents and our Marines not only were of many races but also were representative of many economic classes. Many were poor. Some arrived crammed in the backs of pickups, others by bus. John told me that a lot of parents could not afford the trip.

We in the audience were white and Native American. We were Hispanic, Arab, and African American, and Asian. We were former Marines wearing the scars of battle, or at least baseball caps emblazoned with battles' names. We were Southern whites from

Nashville and skinheads from New Jersey, black kids from Cleveland wearing ghetto rags and white ex-cons with ham-hock forearms defaced by jailhouse tattoos. We would not have been mistaken for the educated and well-heeled parents gathered on the lawns of John's private school a half-year before.

After graduation one new Marine told John, "Before I was a Marine, if I had ever seen you on my block I would've probably killed you just because you were standing there." This was a serious statement from one of John's good friends, a black ex-gang member from Detroit who, as John said, "would die for me now, just like I'd die for him."

My son has connected me to my country in a way that I was too selfish and insular to experience before. I feel closer to the waitress at our local diner than to some of my oldest friends. She has two sons in the

Corps. They are facing the same dangers as my boy. When the guy who fixes my car asks me how John is doing, I know he means it. His younger brother is in the Navy.

Why were I and the other parents at my son's private school so surprised by his choice? During World War II, the sons and daughters of the most powerful and educated families did their bit. If the idea of the immorality of the Vietnam War was the only reason those lucky enough to go to college dodged the draft, why did we not encourage our children to volunteer for military service once that war was done?

Have we wealthy and educated Americans all become pacifists? Is the world a safe place? Or have we just gotten used to having somebody else defend us? What is the future of our democracy when the sons and daughters of the janitors at our elite universities are far more likely to be put in harm's way than are any of the students whose dorms their parents clean?

I feel shame because it took my son's joining the Marine Corps to make me take notice of who is defending me. I feel hope because perhaps my son is part of a future "greatest generation." As the storm clouds of war gather, at least I know that I can look the men and women in uniform in the eye. My son is one of them. He is the best I have to offer. John is my heart.

Oh, how I wish so many of our younger generations could read this article. It makes me so sad to hear the way they talk with no respect for what their fathers, grandfathers and great grandfathers experienced so they can live in freedom. Freedom has been replaced with Free-Dumb.

Cleopatra

By Richard Seal

"Age cannot wither her, nor custom stale
Her infinite variety [...] she makes hungry
Where most she satisfies; for vilest things
Become themselves in her." -
William Shakespeare, Antony and Cleopatra

Cleopatra VII (69 BC – 30 BC) was not only an Egyptian Queen but also the last pharaoh of Ancient Egypt. A member of the Ptolemaic dynasty, she ruled (with her two younger brothers and then her son) for nearly three decades. The woman's **romances and military alliances with Roman leaders Julius Caesar and Mark Antony, alongside her supposed exotic beauty and powers of seduction, have secured her place in world history and popular myth.**

Given that there are no contemporary accounts of Cleopatra's life, there is a lack of certainty about biographical details, although the work of Greco-Roman scholars, particularly Putarch, shed valuable light. She was born in around 69 BC. When her father Ptolemy XII died, in 51 BC, she and her brother Ptolemy XIII became co-regents. The boy's advisers turned him against his sister, and she fled to Syria in AD 49. However, the woman raised an army of mercenaries and returned in AD 48.

Ptolemy XIII had allowed Roman general Pompey to be murdered before Julius Caesar arrived in Alexandria. Cleopatra endeavoured to secure Caesar's military strength and support, reportedly sneaking into the royal palace, and managing to endear herself to him. Ptolemy was overthrown and killed, and his sister was reinstalled to the throne, now alongside her younger brother**, Ptolemy XIV.** Cleopatra gave birth to a son, Caesarion, the following year.

For a time Cleopatra's reign brought some stability and prosperity to the region.
However, in 44 BC, Julius was assassinated. Shortly afterwards the Queen's brother died, and three-year-old **Caesarion** was named co-regent with his mother, as Ptolemy XV. A power struggle soon developed between Mark Anthony and Caesar's adopted son Octavian. Mark began a relationship with the Queen, and they would have three children together.

The antagonism between the two men developed into civil war, and in 31BC, the Egyptian and Roman forces joined to fight Octavian's armies on the west coast of Greece. Cleopatra and Mark Anthony were defeated, and captured in Alexandria in 30BC. With no chance of escape, they took their own lives in August. In one account, the Queen committed suicide by getting a cobra to bite her on the breast. Octavian later had Caesarion strangled, ending the dynasty. Egypt was to become a province of the Roman Empire.

However, the woman has been immortalised by William Shakespeare's play 'Antony and Cleopatra', and the epic 1963 film 'Cleopatra' (starring Elizabeth Taylor and Richard Burton). In addition, her image was shown on Egyptian coins, which was very rare for the historical period.

"She nonetheless survives as a wanton temptress, not the last time a genuinely powerful woman has been transmuted into a shamelessly seductive one." Quote by *Stacy Schiff, Cleopatra: A Life*

The Spanish Neighbours

Terry Tumbler

The Pub Poet's Preamble

"You can try and choose a neighbour
But you can always choose a friend,
A good friend will do a favour,
The other can drive you round the bend!"

The Story Itself

We first became acquainted with our new neighbours a few days after they moved into the house next door up from ours. They were renting it with an 'option to buy' from the owner, Conchi, who had now taken an apartment herself in a nearby city, within easy distance of the local hospital. Her husband was being treated there as an outpatient for a terminal illness, and she was providing regular family support for him, along with her two adult sons.

It was the second house that we had bought on the Costa Blanca, so we regarded it as an informed choice. Located on a small estate on the fringe of a small, Spanish town, all the houses on it are modern and detached.

As a bonus, we are privileged to have a significant number of police families living amongst us, and the estate is patrolled regularly by the local police and the Guardia Civil.

It had been a pleasure living next to Conchi, because her elder son was a professional sportsman, and would regularly lounge around their swimming pool with his friends and a bevy of half-naked beauties. Occasionally they would play ball games together, while standing both ends of their swimming pool.

We could sneak a view of them from a corner of our front bedroom window, the walls surrounding the properties being high. An alternative, better and more discreet view was provided from our tilting en suite bathroom window, but more of that later.

Conchi told us that the person who would now be renting the house was Roberto, who owns (or owned;

who can tell in the present economic crisis?) a small building company. Ana, who we assumed to be his partner, was a voluptuous, natural blond, and was the first to arrive when the house was occupied. She was vigorously sweeping the raised patio adjoining our house when we first said hello. She was keeping her head down and pretending that she hadn't seen us; why, I don't know, but assumed that she was bashful.

She was in her thirties, had very similar features to the Scandinavians, was not skinny but has all the curves in the right places, as I was to find out later (bashful? No way!). We didn't meet Roberto for a further few weeks.
Only a few days into their tenancy, large merchant builder's lorries started rolling up to their gate, and delivering pallets full of bricks, concrete support beams, bags of cement and other materials. As a single storey extension started taking shape on the other side of their property, presumably with the owner's consent, we often left our home to get away from the noise and the dust.
We were getting annoyed, as the swimming pool in our garden began filling up with dirt and had to be cleaned more frequently. One day when relaxing, we even witnessed a lorry-mounted crane swinging pallets in an arc over our pool, which was a dangerous manoeuvre and could easily have caused serious damage. I was on the verge of halting it when the deliveries stopped; fortunately for us, all that they were going to need had been received.

Extensions like this were commonplace, everywhere on the estate; they were illegal, and often built without foundations. Shortly after completion of what turned out to be Roberto's 'Viking-style dining hall', he called me across to admire his latest creation and then asked my unneeded permission to build a similar structure on my side of his house.

The thought of suffering more work was too much and I said politely that he needed approval from the town hall; he said they were not interested in such things and continued pressuring me.

So, having given it some thought, I went to the planning department at the town hall, and told them what he'd told me, using the same words as he'd used, to aggravate them. After all, it didn't mean that what everyone else had done meant that he could follow suit, unopposed.

That same day, the deputy head of the planning department came and inspected his handiwork, asked what else he proposed doing. In view of my strong objection, they took my side and banned him from doing anything else.

In fact, I'd found out by then that there is a regional government agency that deals with town halls that fail to implement planning laws, so I suspect that they were duty bound to take action, in cases of dispute.
That was lucky for my wife really, since I was beginning to wonder what local prison food tasted like, in view of me beginning to weigh up the possibility of shooting the bugger.

Roberto is stocky in a plump sort of way, has a narrow-eyed, impassive, cross-breed Mongolian type of face, and is at least fifteen years older than Ana. He showed no reaction to us after this, but carried on with his normal life; at least, I think it was *his* normal way of behaving. By all appearances, he was a hunting and shooting type of guy, who wore camouflage outfits and drove an ancient four-wheel drive Range Rover with cross-country tyres. I was surprised that he didn't have a feather stuck up his arse, the bloody poser. He now had a lot of time on his hands because the construction industry had all but collapsed; for the Spanish, it was becoming the worst recession in living memory.

One or two days later, he brought home ***the*** dog; it was a mottled brown and cream Pointer, a pedigree gun dog, built like a fully grown greyhound but with floppy ears and a less pointed face. It was led along a long, narrow alley at the back of the house, and locked into a kennel area near the far end, which Roberto had constructed especially for this poor animal.

On the nearside of the alley, is the back wall of the house. There are doors in it leading from the newly built Viking hall and kitchen, and a tall lounge window. On the furthest side of the alley is a long, waist-high plastered brick wall, with wire fence above it, giving a total height of two metres (or 6ft 6"). This gives security from would-be burglars.

Inside the rear boundary wall exists a row of established fir trees, which are occasionally trimmed. These reduce the sunlight that would otherwise shine into the lounge through its back window. They also reduce the width of the alleyway and make it unusable for drying clothes, when the sun is at its height.

Bordering the outside of all our rear gardens is a gravelled walkway, access to which Conchi had provided by inserting a tall, sturdy security gate, which is kept padlocked. The other side of the walkway is a so-called eco park, the hillside of which is covered with evergreen, short hardy trees.

The combined exercise area and tiled-roof open kennel for the dog are barely larger than a small garden shed, and must have been difficult for the dog to turn around in.

Roberto probably had another property elsewhere, because it was not long before he decided to go there for a long weekend. Rather than take the dog with him and Ana, he calculated how much food and water the dog would need for the duration of the holiday, and filled two large bowls with nourishing pellets.

That had to be one hell of a clever dog to realise how much to consume and drink each day, or a fast learner. Roberto himself had a donkey brain, but my darling wife kept telling me that, "We could have had much worse, as a neighbour."

In the Army, when I served as a conscript, an officer like him would've soon had an unpinned grenade rolled into his tent, I can tell you. Bloody moron, he was, without a shadow of doubt.

After day one on its own, the dog started howling, and this continued day and night until Roberto and Ana returned from holiday. I was sorely tempted to complain to the police, but the self-restraint of my other neighbours and, more important, from my overbearing wife, put me off making a rod for our own backs.

The day that they returned, I squared up to Roberto and told him to do something about the howling or else, and he said he would prevent it. His action was to arrange for one or more of his labourers to check on the dog more or less each day, when he was away.

This seemed to be satisfactory to him, so his holidays became more regular and lasted longer. He also showed occasional interest in the dog, and would infrequently take it with him hunting. Unfortunately, the first time he was let loose in the front garden, the dog fled as soon as the vehicle gate was opened, and disappeared down the road in full flight.

It returned hours later, and I saw it waiting outside the empty house. It willingly came with me into our garden, and stretched out contentedly in front of our porch. Later on, I told Ana where it was, and she collected it apologetically, pulling the unwilling dog by its collar back to their house. That was when we found out that the dog's name was Hercules, which I thought was stupid, really, considering its build.

By now, during each holiday break, I was having a laugh as the birds helped themselves to the food pellets and occasionally dropped them on our rear garden too. As I expected, the scheduled visits by Roberto's muppet morons to see his dog also became less frequent.

I once saw those who had assumed responsibility for its welfare covering their faces with scarves, to combat the odours coming from the kennel, from which 'Hercules' was refusing to budge. The following day, I saw it prancing around eagerly in the back of their old car as they took it away. I got some satisfaction from knowing that the car must have stunk like hell afterwards, and Hercules disappeared from the scene for a long time.

Peace settled on us, and Roberto began improving the house that he had not yet bought. The front garden, primarily the pool area, was lit like Blackpool, with red, green and yellow flood lights illuminating the front from their upstairs solarium. To these were added self-illuminating poolside lights that had spears on top that could transfix any unwary, slipping soul.

I waited to see if he was expecting any vampires amongst his visitors, waiting for someone to get impaled, or for children to arrive that he didn't like.

The one side of the pool that was too close to the outside garden wall was filled with earth, and grass seeds were planted in it; I wondered how long it would take to turn into liquid mud when it rained, since no drainage holes were drilled into any of the retaining walls, and the floor was fully tiled. Failing that unavoidable event, anyone who lay on the grass, or placed a towel on top, would

probably get eaten alive by the large ants that would be nesting in the soil below. He had no brains, that man.
Just before the season changed and autumn beckoned, the pain-in-the-arse decided to throw his first fiesta. The first we knew of it was when traditional flamenco caterwauling started blasting out at full volume.

We were woken by the sudden noise, and rushed from the front garden porch to the back area of the house, to sit more peacefully on our loungers, where we then got covered in smoke from the metal chimney that he had erected at the back of the Viking hall.
Mind you, the smell of roasting piglet was wonderful, but we had no false hopes that we were going to taste any of it.

As guests arrived in ever increasing numbers, so the volume of their laughter and talking began to match that coming from the loudspeakers perched in the Viking hall. It only subsided when the pig was being consumed, as we could hear from the pig-like grunting noises coming from him and his guests.

Next thing, we heard the sound of a child bawling at full blast, so went upstairs to see what the problem was. A boy was holding his (literally) bleeding side, and being led naked to the waiting would-be family nurses, howling for all he was worth. I couldn't make my mind up if the child was re-enacting a scene from the crucifixion, or was genuinely hurt after falling in the pool, or had lanced himself on one of Robby boy's light fittings.

Whatever the cause of the ruckus, peace descended and we went back downstairs. We agreed to stay indoors, instead of continuing to suffer from smoke inhalation.
As darkness descended, the strobe effects of the lighting, in time with the music, was magnificent, I had to admit. They also started playing Euro rock, culminating in a Spanish version of the Birdy song and dancing in a drunken circle, flapping their arms as wings.

It was a pity that Roberto's guests failed to take action when he was prancing around like a pheasant, and had not shot him with one of the shotguns that he left lying around.

In the course of time, we found that we could afford to be indulgent with these family fiestas, because they only tended to take place once or twice a year, and finished before midnight.

That first year, as I had predicted, the metal chimney broke in half during a high wind and Roberto never bothered to mend it; no doubt he knew that if he did, it would break again, him being so bad a builder. I could also see that the cement rendering on the extension was cracking and loosening from the bricks underneath.

Ana began learning to swim in their pool, as we witnessed upstairs after hearing what appeared to be a baby hippo struggling in the water. As she got better at it, aided by arm bands, the splashing decreased. She also had an uninhibited way of drying out, by lying spread-eagled on her back, stark naked, with only a beach towel separating her bronzing body from the heat reflecting, glazed tiles underneath.

I thought of offering her one of our surplus, faded, sun loungers to use, but decided not to, in case she suspected me of spying on her from our bathroom window. Later, I was glad that I hadn't, after she started to spread her legs as well, facing me, since it would have been difficult for her to do that on a lounger.

As autumn approached, it was not uncommon to see Ana swimming starker's in the pool, using the breast stroke and going great strides from one end to the other. After a while, Roberto felt the urge to join her, stripped off his trunks and, beneath his domed belly, revealing a miniscule, pencil-sized dick.

I chortled and ducked back, as his head snapped up, looking for the source of the noise. Clearly he was under-endowed, so I understood at last why they slept in separate bedrooms, and why she spent so much time expending her energy on daily, desperate sprints around the estate.

At least, I am fairly confident that was the explanation for their lack of public affection; he already had a son in his twenties, who I met when Roberto was planning his second extension to the house, so he was presumably divorced, and we were correct in assuming that Ana was his mistress.

Soon, we were offered another distraction less to my liking: Hercules had returned, together with two absolutely delightful puppy Pointers. Ana thought so too, since she looked up at me on one of those rare occasions when I was watching this entertainment from an upstairs side window, and smiled affectionately at me and then lovingly at the dogs.

All three of them were ushered by her into the kennel at the end of the narrow alley, and there they stayed for a while. It was only a short while, because all three started barking loudly whenever anyone walked past using the rear path; they would poke their heads between the branches of the pine trees and frighten whoever was passing. Great fun it was to them, but as noisy as hell for Ana, let alone us neighbours.

To reduce the noise, Ana kept the kennel gate open after that, giving them the run of the alley. The drawback was that there were now three dogs crapping at will, and the workload associated with clearing it grew and grew as the dogs got bigger and bigger; first it had to be brushed into heaps (if the excrement was reasonably solid), then shovelled into plastic bags; then, the floor had to be washed down with disinfectant and the dogs allowed back into the alley. The process had to be repeated on an almost daily basis.

On occasion, the puppies would sieve through the uncollected heaps of crap to find anything useful that they had already eaten that could be consumed again. Overall, it was stomach churning fun for the onlooker, and I brought out my Olympus camera to take some memorable pictures; one of them is shown next.

Roberto played his part as well, no doubt at Ana's insistence, to demonstrate that he was not deficient in all departments. However, he would take shortcuts: rather than deposit the deposits in plastic bags, for disposal in the Dog Poo bins near the centre of the estate, he would open the metal gate leading to the footpath at the rear, then use the rubber flat-ended shovel he had brought with him to lob the excrement over the other side of the footpath.

know this because I often saw the blade rising, and the heaps catapulting overhead as he worked in double quick time to complete this unwanted task, before he was found out. I never managed to photo him doing this, because it was earlier than eight o'clock in the morning when he did it, and I found it a real effort to get up that early.

Likewise, Roberto had a longer-term interest in training his two future gun-dogs, so he would let all three out of their prison, to run at lightning speed across the footpath and then onto the slopes of the eco park outside the estate.

There he would stand, pointlessly waving his arms in various directions and barking inaudible instructions, as the dogs ignored him. They didn't have a clue what they were supposed to do, and the situation stayed the same all the times that I watched them at play.

Once, I opened the shutters on the rear landing window, to see Roberto advancing into chest-high grass, bending down and grasping what looked like a large hare. He held this creature by its rear legs, and I thought he was going to larrup it, but instead he simply tossed it into the air.

It cartwheeled as it looped at least twenty feet away from him, and it was only when it yelped that I realised that it was one of the puppies. The dog picked itself up, unhurt, and ran as if for its life. Roberto tried for days to get it to come anywhere near him. It only ran past him when it was forced to return to its home in the alley, when he would give it a reassuring pat on the head.

Roberto and Ana soon resumed taking long and short holidays, filling the two large bowls with food pellets and water as thought necessary. Shortly afterwards, the vultures descended and flew away with what they wanted. Getting desperately short of food and water, the agile and taller Hercules decided to take matters into his own paws.

He leapt up and used his teeth to grab a hose looped in the taller branches of the trees. It was attached to an open standpipe, and he ripped the plastic nozzle off the hose, to give him and the puppies' fresh access to a non-stop supply of water. Eventually this poured into my back garden, which was the first that I knew of it.

We had no contact phone number to warn Roberto what had happened, nor could I get into the property to turn off the standpipe, with the three dogs growling at me When he came back later that night, he would undoubtedly face a large water bill, and a huddle of three dogs at the highest dry section of the alley, near the Viking hall. At least it had been cleared of crap, to a degree. Most of it would have accumulated in the kennel that the three dogs were now sharing.

Now it got even more entertaining. As the puppies grew taller and became leggier, so they became sexually involved. I wondered at first what all the noise was, frequently hearing throaty growls and high pitched whines. On checking from an upstairs window, I could see that one of the puppies was a bitch, and the two males were taking it in turns to mount her.

I began to appreciate how Hercules had earned his name, and wondered if the next generation of puppies would turn out to be mottled or all-brown, and what would be the effect of in-breeding if they were all-brown. This seemed to be taking place without the knowledge or interest of either Roberto or Ana, who were out most of each day.

It was happening so often that the poor bitch eventually resorted to protecting her vulnerable rear end, by reversing into the hedge and thrusting it against the outside wall; only her head was visible, and the two male dogs walked aimlessly back and forth, looking baffled at the unwillingness of this no doubt highly appealing young bitch to cooperate with them.

One thing I have noticed about pointers is the lack of intelligence in their vacuous eyes, but for all I know the same could apply to Roberto, who gazes at life through slits above his aquiline nose. It wouldn't have surprised me to find out that he was cross-eyed.

Once, when work was at last presented to him, he had to cut metal sheets into long strips; he used a round cutter to do this, placing the supported metal on his patio, next to our house and in full (but unseen) view of me. As he cut each strip with the circular saw, a sheet of flame leapt backwards, towards his trouser bottoms.
Watching him was one of his younger workers, and both of us got really alarmed as the flames engulfed not just his lower legs but the cable driving the circular saw. He ignored or was unaware of this, but when the younger worker took his turn, he stood at a totally different angle and no part of him was touched by the flames. Roberto took his turn and continued as before. The man is as thick as a brush.

Ana began staying at home after a while, and resumed her running, swimming and sun bathing. She also took infrequent pity on the dogs, allowing them access to the front garden via the Viking hall.

One day, as I was reading in our front porch, an almighty commotion broke out next door; I could hear her sobbing and crying out something like '¡Madre Mia!', a lot of scuffling and running, and the dogs yelping as a repeated bopping sound could be heard.
I ran upstairs, looked through the bathroom window, and saw a nude Ana, distraught and furious, chasing the dogs with a rolled up girly magazine, and bopping them with it whenever she caught one of them.
'Bop, bop, bop!' came the blows, fast and furious, with her jumping into the pool at intervals, to snatch a break and cleanse herself, then jumping out with renewed

mental energy to resume the onslaught, while clutching her pussy.

Putting two and two together and possibly making five: when I looked at the really crumpled large bathing towel, I got the feeling that she had got caught napping, so to speak, by one of the pups enjoying licking her.

This was backed up by her behaviour; crouching and mouthing Spanish obscenities (I have more than a smattering of Spanglish at my disposal), with her frequently grasping her crotch, or waving her arms like a windmill before continuing to 'Bop a pup'.

After a further spell of screaming, she let the three of them have access to the alley, into which they sped jet-propelled. Afterwards, the molested Ana limped into the house and got scrubbed and dressed.

Unaware of any of this, Roberto brought home that evening four short, broad-leafed sapling trees and planted them in the narrow strip of shallow grass-topped earth, next to the pool. "Fine", I smiled sickly. "So now he's going to clog the pool filter with leaves."

Not much later, Roberto decided against buying the house, but agreed with Conchi that he would act as her resident agent and sell it for her. It was a successful arrangement and contracts were quickly exchanged a couple of months later with a young couple, who behave normally and are as quiet as church mice, although the husband soon ripped up the poolside trees and laid artificial grass.

They too have a dog, but it is a miniature and stays in the house with them. Occasionally too, they look after a Golden Labrador on behalf of close relatives, which stays at the end of the alley and howls most nights as if the area is haunted.

Neither Roberto nor Ana bade their farewells to the neighbours, but you can see that they live in our memories. By the way, the Viking Hall began to collapse.

***

Dogs are welcome in this hotel.
We never had a dog that smoked in bed and set fire to the blankets. We never had a dog that stole our towels and played the T.V. too loud, or had a noisy fight with his traveling companion. We never had a dog that got drunk and broke up the furniture....So if your dog can vouch for you, you're welcome too. The Management

Man's Best Friend

Trudie Oakley

Christopher Harmer tugged on the huge dog's lead, but the dog was going nowhere. The kennel owner came to his rescue and with a little persuasion and the bribe of a dried pigs ear Nikademus was eventually loaded into the waiting Land Rover. "Take it easy with him er.."

"Jude just call me Jude."

Christopher had been orphaned at the age of six when his parents had been killed as their coach had plunged into a ravine in Spain. He had been staying with his Grandparents at the time and fortunately they were able to continue giving him the love and security that every well balanced child needs. Unfortunately, maybe brought on by the loss of her only son Grandma succumbed to dementia and his world was turned upside down when Grandpa died suddenly leaving no-one to care for him. His only other living relative, a maiden aunt, had settled somewhere in South Africa but little was known of her whereabouts.

He had been taken into care at the age of nine and passed from one foster home to another, each stay shorter than the one before as his behaviour deteriorated. Eventually he left the chaos that was the care system and lived contentedly if not happily in a bed sit working in the offices of a well known supermarket where he liked to be known as Jude – he thought it sounded cool. He much preferred that to Christopher – that name belonged to a long abandoned little boy who he wanted to forget.

He avoided close contacts of any sort having learnt that buttoning down emotions was the only way to protect oneself from hurt. He never looked to the future, had no desire to explore the big wide world; just lived from day to day keeping everything and everyone at a distance.

Then, out of the blue, he had learnt that his aunt, who unbeknown to him had by now moved to the Scottish Highlands, had died some months before and, as he was her only living relative, she had left her entire estate to him with just one proviso. He had to take care of Nikademus, her three year old Mastif. So here he was driving to her large draughty house in her large powerful car with a decidedly unwanted large dog.

When they reached the house the dog immediately ran to his mistresses' room whimpering. "No good you looking in there you dope. She's gone and left you, just like everyone does." He threw down a bowl of food "You can eat that or not, I couldn't care less."

Man and dog reached an uneasy truce over the next few weeks and when Jude took himself off for a walk Nikademus followed behind, just as he had always done with his beloved mistress. It had been raining heavily for the past two weeks but today was dry although the sky was dark overhead and there was a cold wind blowing. He loved this weather; it suited his mood, dark and cold. As usual the dog tagged along and he began to wonder how long he would have to put up with him before he could give him away without jeopardizing his inheritance.

The stream that ran nearby was very lively, far more like a river now as it crashed over the rocks throwing spray that was blown away in an instant. He walked into the water fascinated as it raced to the top of his wellingtons drenching his socks. It was freezing. He turned back to the bank but slipped, this was not funny; he was drenched. While he was scrabbling to regain a foothold his legs were taken from under him by a broken branch which pushed him further and further downstream, and the water here was quite a bit deeper; he was scared now. He tried to stay on his feet but the force of the water kept knocking him down. It was so cold and he was getting weaker. He was fully immersed now and there seemed to be some contra current pulling him down. Struggling to keep his head above water he was vaguely aware of Nikademus barking and running along the bank, but he went under again. It was so cold but he couldn't fight any more – no strength – too cold. He hadn't expected to die today. What a surprise – he never thought it would end like this.

Suddenly he felt an excruciating pain which jolted him back to consciousness. He opened his eyes to see his arm lodged in the great dog's mouth. His saviour lay astride a fallen tree which was half in the water and he was holding onto his master for dear life. Realising what the dog had done Jude felt an enormous rush of gratitude towards him, and was relieved beyond measure to be out of danger. With his free hand he grabbed hold of a broken branch and seeing this, the dog let go freeing him to haul himself toward the log using both arms. He moved along the tree grabbing hold of jutting

branches until eventually he managed to draw himself out of the water and stagger onto the bank before collapsing exhausted.
After a few minutes he sat up and saw Nikademus looking his way seemingly entreating him for help but then he turned his great head away and lay it back onto the log as if realising that none was coming. That was when Jude saw blood running from beneath the dog and mingling with the still frothing water.
For the first time in his adult life Jude felt emotion. This clever dog had saved his life and the thought of him now being in distress was almost more than he could bear. With renewed adrenalin fuelled strength he worked his way along the log until he reached the dog. "Don't worry boy. I've got you. You're going to be fine." He would never know how he did it but he hoisted Nikademus out of danger and tramped across the fields to home, laying him gently on the back seat of his car and thanking heaven that the keys were still in it. It took half an hour to get to the vet and all the while he was talking to the dog who lay deathly still with his eyes closed. "You'll be alright boy. Just hang on now. We'll get you sorted in no time – don't you dare die on me now!"
Covered in blood and still ringing wet a wild man ran into Stace's veterinary practice shouting for someone to help his dog. All hands jumped to and in no time Nikademus was stretchered into theatre as Jude was handed a cup of strong coffee and quizzed as to how the pair of them had got into such a state.

Once his arm had been examined Jude was persuaded to drive to the local clinic where his wound was dressed and he was pumped full of antibiotics, and as he began once again to explain how he had come by the bite, without warning, he began to cry. Years of pent up emotion poured from him like water through a sieve. All the grief and resentment he had kept inside bubbled over and into his consciousness just as the water in the stream had bubbled into his wellingtons, and the tears just would not stop. The doctor on call decided to sedate him and keep him in overnight; it was obvious that he was in no fit state to make his own way home.

When Jude visited Nikademus the next day his heart leapt to see him alive and well, and the joy he felt at the wagging tail that acknowledged his presence was almost overwhelming. Apparently the poor fellow had been unable to move from the fallen tree as he had dislocated his shoulder, probably in the effort of holding Jude against the pressure of the water, and he had also sustained a nasty tear across his abdomen which was now sutured and dressed. The dog, like Jude would need a course of antibiotics but all being well would be able to go home with his master tomorrow.

Jude leant against the desk admiring the pretty receptionist and wondering if she had a boyfriend. She smiled at him "Now sir, if I could just take a few details starting with your name."

"It's Christopher, Christopher Harmer and my dog's name is Nikademus."

Six months after your dog passes you still can't bear to talk about her. Yet, some may say "she was just a dog."
You reach under the bed and stumble across an old toy of hers and burst into tears. Yet, she was just a dog.
After a long and mentally draining day at work, you'd give anything to come home and just cuddle with her. Yet, she was just a dog.
Those who never owned one, will never get it. That dog was your friend, cuddle buddy, jogging partner, playmate, anxiety reliever, guard dog, alarm clock, etc....

Just a dog, right?

–Emily Perez

Observations on Growing Older:

The things you used to care to do, you no longer care to do, but you really do care that you don't care to do them anymore.

Scene Unseen

By Richard Seal

Catherine had been a believer in living life to the full, always caring, sharing words of wisdom and joy, revelling in laughter and love. Her husband, Dan, watched his wife slipping away in her hospital bed, teetering between life and death. His thoughts about her, fevered, twist turned with feelings flipping between darkness and intermittent light into a place of stillness, peace and release. He knew that Catherine was not looking to enter a tunnel with the gates of Heaven at its end, she had had no desire to hear any celestial voices calling her forward. She had told him not to expect to see her floating above her body any time soon. He felt her fingers' feeling faltering, ragged breathing fading finally, before she took a silent step into a scene unseen.

Linda felt that her mum had barely remained in that space in her final few hours. It was the same face there in the hospital bed, but her essence was already displaced, departed, and her form had been replaced by a half-stranger. There was some calmness for a while with smile fragments, recognition half recalled, before the glimmers stuttered then stalled. In the last few seconds of enveloping darkness, it had seemed as if mum

was able to disengage from the pain with an expression focused beyond, aglow. At the end, her brow was smooth, all the fear and suffering had gone. Linda knew that she must have sensed their love in the room as she drifted freely, then softly let go. At last awake, she arrived.

Under strict instructions, Catherine's funeral is humanistic and black clothes are banned. Prayers are not required or desired, and hymns are nowhere to be seen. Upbeat songs lift spirits a little, while the speeches adopt a lightness of touch, focusing on celebration in tributes to the woman's vitality, passion, and sense of humour. Her family and friends give thanks for better places which were created in their lives by her touch. Despite his grief, Dan manages a little smile. He squeezes Linda's hand, catches her eye, and hopes she can also see her mum's grin and an eyebrow arched above a big glass of wine. Catherine had warned that a church send-off would see her taking a swing at the vicar, aiming a wild kick at the pulpit, knocking over the font, and hanging around to haunt them all forever ...

Empathy...a lonely little word
with a strong meaning.
Big you can see it, as you can small
But not empathy.
Although you can feel it

You can say there is a lot of water
But not empathy of water.
It is possible for a pail to have a leak
But not an empathy.
A car can go fast
But it cannot go empathy.

Empathy has a singular meaning
But to achieve that
it needs a friendly word
to explain why.
Mum can have empathy
But we need to say to whom.
The tyrant had empathy
But we need to say why.

Empathy...awareness of feeling
The emotional link between people
The feeling of love and
understanding between couples

Empathy a lonely strong little word that means so much...

Story Telling Twelve

Best Served Cold

Trudie Oakley

As soon as he enquired after George Foster the demeanour of the erstwhile friendly café owner changed and he pushed back the money proffered by the stranger in exchange for a cup of tea, "Take yer money and get out." He lowered his voice and leant towards the unwelcome stranger, "Any friend of that bastard is not welcome in here now or at any time. Now sling yer hook before I lose my temper."

Feeling a little shamefaced he picked up his money and left under the glare of several sets of eyes and as he closed the door a harsh voice rang out "Get yourself down to Len's where your sort belongs and I hope whatever you eat chokes you." So; it seems the George Foster of old is still just as much of a low life as he ever was. The stranger stuck his hands in his pockets and with a wry smile wandered down the road a little further crossing over onto a small recreation area and settling down on a bench directly opposite Len's greasy spoon.

It was almost as he remembered it from twenty years ago although perhaps now in need of a little maintenance. The white painted windows were flaking badly and above the door the word Len's, hand painted in a faded red, confirmed the owner of the establishment. Grubby net curtains, which had probably at one time been white covered the bottom half of the windows, no doubt to prevent the attention of unwelcome prying eyes from witnessing whatever shady goings on occurred inside.

Story Telling Twelve

As he sat relaxed in the dappled sunlight Simon Mead let his mind drift back to that awful day when his best friend Danny had died in his arms. Most of his young life he had been a loner ill at ease in his surroundings having little in common with most of his neighbours, and having to attend the local Secondary school had only served to increase his sense of isolation. The majority of his fellow students had absolutely no interest in education as most of them, like him, came from families that existed on benefit and the odd bit of pilfering and could see no good reason to change the status quo. Danny's arrival was a turning point for Simon as here was a like-minded boy who aspired to get on in the world and who realised that a good education was the necessary key for success.

Danny's English father had been an electrical engineer and had met Jessy when working in Jamaica. They had married and eventually returned to England with Danny, their only son, but soon after their arrival Mr Bristow had caught influenza and succumbed to the Pneumonia which had rapidly ensued. As a result of her husband's death Jessy Bristow had looked for and found work as a doctor's receptionist and moved with Danny into a council flat close by, the move resulting in Danny changing schools and befriending Simon. The two had got on like a house on fire and Jessy, relieved that Danny had settled and found a good friend, had welcomed Simon into her home so that in a very short time she was calling him her second son. Unlike his own home Jessy's flat was an oasis of love and comfort.

Every day after school they would spread out their books on her dining table and work in silence until she came home. The flat often smelled of something appetising cooking slowly in the oven and there was always homemade cake and tea waiting for them, and soon after she got in from work dinner would be served. All this was a complete contrast to Simon's own home where the only food on offer would be oven chips or frozen pizzas, and that was of course self service. Rather than preparing a meal his mother would be opening a bottle or entertaining her latest boyfriend. It was safe to say that neither Simon nor his little sister Gwen were on her list of priorities.

Gwen was ten years younger than Simon; they were half siblings and neither of them would ever really know for sure who their fathers were but despite, or maybe because of their constant neglect, they had a formed an unbreakable bond. He well remembered how he had worried about Gwen as a tiny baby. At the age of ten he was still a child himself but had taken on the responsibility of filling Gwen's bottles and changing her nappy when their mother had passed out too drunk to hear her baby's crying. Often they would be left alone until the early hours and he would carefully carry Gwen into his bed and snuggle up with her. He had liked those times. It was good to have someone to cuddle and feel close to and paradoxically, with his volatile mother absent, they were the only times he really felt safe.

He found he was balling his fists as he thought of the waste of space that was his mother. He wondered what she was doing now, probably still careering through life in a drunken haze –

he hated her, but that was all in the past; he had a good life now and that was all that mattered.

His mind returned to the day Danny died – the reason he was here now. It had been a cold Autumnal day and they had been walking home hunched into their coats, talking and laughing, looking forward to getting into the warm. They hadn't noticed the gang of boys that had been following them until Danny suddenly fell to the ground. The boys surrounded the pair and it was George Foster, the school thug and bully boy, who spoke. "Well if it ain't the two teachers' pets." He kicked Danny who was still on the ground, "Get up blackie. You should be up in one of them trees over there. What you got in yer bag – bananas?" The rest of the boys laughed – George had to be appeased.

"Leave him alone Foster. You're a big man with all the gang around you but let's see you stand on your own feet; come and fight me – come on, just you and me." Simon was shaking with fear and could not believe what he had just heard himself say, but he was angry too. He stepped toward Foster but was stopped short when a large knife was thrust in his face.

"Come on then teacher's pet. Come and get a bit of this, let's see how brave you are now."

Before Simon could react Danny had pushed him aside eyes glaring, he slammed into Foster who stumbled backward. "Put that knife down and then we can see how brave **you** are. Let's just show all your friends here what a big man you are – or are you just a stupid spineless bully after all."

For a second Foster was speechless then, face contorted he roared "I ain't having no nig-nog calling me names. You fucking black bastard, I'll show you who's a coward." Before anyone could react he had plunged the knife into Danny who cried out as he fell to the ground. For a few seconds everyone was rooted to the spot shaken to the core by what they had just witnessed. Foster turned to Simon and waved the bloody knife in his face, "If you say anything about this it's your turn next, and then that little sister of yours – get it, and I hope the black bastard dies." He bent to wipe his knife on Danny's trousers "Come on lads, let's get out of here," he smirked waving the knife, "Last one to the café gets this up his arse."

Simon stared after the running pack scarcely able to understand what had just happened. He snapped back to attention when Danny tried to sit up and groaned. Under his coat his shirt was fast turning red and Simon suddenly became really afraid for his friend. "Don't move Danny," he sat on the ground and cradled his friend's head in his lap. Several people gathered round to help and he was aware of a man saying he had called for help. He patted Simon on the shoulder "An ambulance is on its way son, don't worry now they'll soon sort your friend out."

Danny looked up, his eyes full of tears. "It hurts Si and I'm cold, really cold. Tell mum where I've gone, she'll be worried." His eyes closed and Simon watched as tears ran down his cheeks. He shucked off his coat and covered his friend.

"They'll be here soon Danny, won't be long now," but in his heart he knew that his friend was dead.

Simon went in the ambulance to the hospital but there was no siren, no life or death rush; Danny was gone. In shock he was taken to a small room where someone brought him a cup of tea and said a doctor would be along shortly just to make sure he was ok. He looked down at his blood soaked sleeves in silence and sat immobile watching a skin form on his tea as it turned cold. He didn't know how long he'd sat staring at the cup and didn't bother to look up when the door opened. He smelt her perfume first then leapt from his seat when he saw Jessy standing in the doorway and ran into her arms. They clung together wrapped in grief. A mother had lost her only son, a boy had lost his only true friend and both were inconsolable.

Fearing for his sister Simon had kept silent, telling the police that a gang of boys unknown to him had swooped on them and knifed Danny just because he was black. He was riddled with guilt and hated himself for his cowardice and so many times had so nearly told the truth but if anything happened to Gwen he knew he could never ever forgive himself. Life had been really difficult for him since that day and the change in Jessy, who had been a beautiful statuesque woman was pitiful to see. Now it was Simon who would make sure that she ate. He would collect Gwen from school then go on to Jessys' to cook dinner for the three of them; in fact they all but moved in, just returning to their own flat to sleep.

His school work had taken a steep down turn and as a result he had left school at the earliest opportunity with no qualifications taking on a succession of menial jobs so that he could continue to take care of Gwen and Jessy. Gradually

Jessy began to regain her strength both mental and physical, so much so that one evening when they had finished dinner Jessy broached the subject that had been on her mind for some time. "Simon, I've been thinking." The timbre of her voice made both he and Gwen sit up. "You will be eighteen next month and as far as I can see you've no prospects – just going from one dead end job to another." She held up a hand to silence Simon before he could speak, "Now, you're a very clever boy and but for losing my Danny you would have done well for yourself – yes or no?"

Simon hesitated "Well yes, I suppose I would have tried to get into university or tech school but …."

"There are no buts Simon, we both went downhill for a while and no mistake, but now we've got to climb back up to where we belong – yes?" She asked the question with arched eyebrows, "So I think you should join the army, that way you could get right away from here and I know for a fact that you could get a good education if you showed promise and I know you are full to the brim with promise." She raised her hand for silence once again, "I know the first thing you are going to say is that you can't leave little Gwen here, and rightly so, but how about this! Gwen can live with me permanently so neither of us will be alone. I want to leave this place and the awful memories too so I have applied for two jobs that are miles away from here, and I know I can get excellent references from work as I've already asked. If we moved Gwen could go to a good school so that she can make something of herself too – what do you say to all that?"

Simon and Gwen looked at each other wide eyed, Jessy was right, they were all going nowhere. Simon had thrown away chances and Gwen's prospects at the local school were limited to say the least, but what appealed most to Simon was the opportunity for all of them to get away from the likes of George Foster who was already treading the predicted path in life that fate had ordained for him as a lazy low-life thug. It hadn't taken long for all of them to agree that opportunity was knocking on their door and Simon smiled to himself when Jessy had miraculously produced a pamphlet detailing careers on offer in the army and how to apply for them. She was quite a woman.

So it had come to pass that Jessy and Gwen moved to Brighton and both had thrived in their new surroundings. Fifteen years on Jessy was newly retired and Gwen was in her third year at Bristol University, now a beautiful and confident young woman. Simon had joined the army and excelled. He had progressed rapidly and loved his life in the elite special service until being wounded which meant that he could no longer continue on active duty, and as a desk job did not appeal to him he had accepted an invitation to join her majesty's secret service working under deep cover. He was now on an assignment in the area and although Foster was not part of his mission the opportunity to get even at last was just too good to miss.

Simon snapped back into the present when the door to Len's opened and three men came out. His heart turned in his chest as he recognised George Foster. Although now a man there was no mistaking the deep set eyes and wide flat head that sat over that short bull neck. His black hair was cut short and greased down. He hadn't gained much in height since they were boys but he was heavily muscled now, probably Simon thought from working out. It was all he could do not to attack his prey there and then, but now he had him in his sights he could wait.

The advantages of his current profession had given him access to all the information he needed to study his subject in depth. He had learnt that Foster was the proprietor of a building firm which was actually just a front to cover his more nefarious dealings and that his yard was just a stone's throw from the housing estate where they had both grown up. He watched Foster bid goodbye to his two companions and drive off, "Bye you piece of shit. I'll be seeing you later." He crossed the road and entered Len's café. His unkempt down at heel appearance suited the place well, "Cup of tea and a bacon sandwich when you're ready please."

Looking the stranger up and down Len acknowledged his request and pointed to a table by the window, "I'll bring it over."

Simon had waited the day out knowing that Foster was a creature of habit and called into his yard every evening. Dusk was falling as he watched his quarry get out of his sign written van to unlock the padlocked yard gates and drive in. Once inside he closed and locked up again looking all around as he did so. Simon smiled to himself; obviously vigilance was a necessity for those living a life of crime. There was a prefabricated building tucked in the far corner of the yard and he watched as Foster entered and a light appeared in the bare window. He scaled the chain link fence with ease and made his way silently to the building and tried the door - it was open.

Foster who had been sitting at a desk strewn with bundles of money, sensed movement and swung round to face his intruder. "What the hell!" he tried to get to his feet but Simon pushed him back into his chair and pinioned him for the few seconds that it took to tie him with the rope that he had brought for the purpose. Having secured the upper body he looped the rope around thrashing legs so that his victim was trussed well and truly and unable to move.

Foster's face was a kaleidoscope of fear, anger and outrage. "What the 'ell do you think you're doing? You won't get away with this, you don't know who you're dealing with do yer." He changed tack, "Look if you want the money just take it and piss off, I'll ……."

"You'll what? You'll let me go and won't come looking for me? I don't think so, and anyway I'm not here for money."

"What the hell do yer want then you bastard. Who the 'ell are yer anyway? You look like a bloody tramp but……"

"That goes with the job Foster, but what I really want is to hear you say how sorry you are for killing my friend Danny – you know, nig-nog I think you called him."

Foster creased his forehead trying to understand then realisation dawned, "You're that bloody kid from school, the teacher's pet who knocked around with a darkie." He bristled, "Well I ain't saying sorry for nothing, as far as I'm concerned I done the world a favour." He was angry now, "I've 'ad enough of this, just untie me and piss off, or else."

"It will have to be or else I'm afraid." Taking out a knife Simon slit open a leg of Foster's trousers and sliced into his thigh. Blood poured from the wound.

Shocked almost beyond words Foster cried out "Oh for God's sake! What the 'ell have you done?"

"I've cut your femoral artery which means that you will bleed to death in very short order," Simon held up a piece of rope, "Unless I apply this tourniquet to stop it, but before I do I want to hear you beg for forgiveness and say you're sorry for killing Danny and being such a worthless low life."

Foster was really scared now. He was sitting in a pool of blood and urine "Okay, okay. I'm sorry I ever hurt your friend and I'm beggin yer now so for God's sake tie that bloody rope round my leg you..."

"It's no good calling on God old son and you didn't hurt my friend - you killed him. I would imagine he felt just like you do right now – are you getting cold."

"I'm beggin yer." Foster nodded toward the money on his desk, "Take all that money, I promise I won't come after yer." He was shouting now, "Take what yer want but tie that bloody rope round my leg. I'm sorry alright, I'm sorry, sorry, sorry for killing your friend," he looked at Simon now with pleading eyes "Please mate, just finish this now, I've said I'm sorry."

Simon moved to stand behind Foster, "Okay if that's what you want I'll finish it." He took his victim's head into his arms and snapped his neck just as he had been trained to do. Sighing he picked up several bundles of money and stuffed them into his pockets – shouldn't look a gift horse in the mouth and all that.

He left as silently as he had arrived and walked away in the shadows. He was neither sad nor elated. He had taken his revenge and it was true what they said, it is a dish best served cold.

****

Family and Friends

My family and friends

Supported me in a cleanse

When my world was dark

They ignited a spark

When I was down

They changed my frown

I learned to smile

It took a while

My darkness came to an end

Because of my family and friends

Sarah Dawkins

Humour Corner....

SINGLES AD ....

This has to be one of the best singles ads ever printed. It appeared in The Atlanta Journal.

SINGLE BLACK FEMALE seeks male Companionship, ethnicity unimportant. I'm a very good looking girl who LOVES to play. I love long walks in the woods, riding in your pickup truck, hunting, camping and fishing trips, cozy winter nights lying by the fire. Candlelight dinners will have me eating out of your hand. I'll be at the front door when you get home from work, wearing only what nature gave me. Call (xxx) xxx-xxxx and ask for Daisy.

Over 15,000 men found themselves talking to the Atlanta RSPCA about an 8-week old black Labrador retriever.

The First World War
Largest Prisoners Escape

July 24 1918, Holzminden–In September 1917, a new PoW camp opened in Holzminden for British officers; other camps had become overcrowded as the war progressed and more officers were captured from the counterattacks around Passchendaele.

Among their number was James Whale, who would later go on to direct Frankenstein and Bride of Frankenstein. The camp commandant quickly acquired a reputation for cruelty; some prisoners were killed, and others (such as the famous Capt. Leefe Robinson) were kept in continuous solitary confinement.

Within weeks, many of the officers were planning an escape attempt, digging a long tunnel out of the camp with spoons and whatever tools they could steal.

They were aided in the task by three Germans, two men who were bribed (the commandant did not treat his own men well, either), and one woman who was infatuated with one of the prisoners. Those who weren't digging worked on the ventilation system, or prepared papers and clothes for after the escape.

By July, the tunnel was finally finished, and around 100 of the 700 men in the camp were set to go through the tunnel to freedom in the small hours of July 24th. Those who had done the majority of the digging went through first. Unfortunately, the tunnel collapsed on the 30th man, who had to be pulled out; the escape attempt ended there. The alarm was raised by a nearby farmer, who noticed his fields being trampled by the escapees.

Nineteen of the officers were rounded up and returned to Holzminden, but ten were able to make it safely to the Netherlands. One of them, Col. Rathbone, was proficient enough in German to travel by rail and made out of the country in only five days; the others had to travel by foot and took multiple weeks.

The Photo above: The remains of the tunnel, fully dug up by the Germans after the escape attempt.

LATE AFTERNOON
Lin Penhaul

"Heaven is a sandy beach with room to sunbathe"
That's what my city dwelling friends tell me, but as I walked I saw things differently.
The late afternoon sun felt warm on my face and the slight breeze brought a salty tang to my tongue.
I could tell without looking that the tide was about half-way out.
Neither the thrusting slap of high tide nor the pebble-dragging grind of low tide could be heard, only the gentle ripple of the slack.

Little whorls on the damp sand told of lugworms trying to hide from the early morning bait –diggers. Curving lines of pebbles dredged from the ocean, smoothly contoured in witness to the harsh passage marked the tide line, their browns, creams and pearly whites dulling as they dried.
Still pools under slimy green rocks provided home for tiny soft-shelled crabs scurrying out of sight as any threatening shadow appeared on the water.

Overhead gulls swooped and cried, cutting the sky into segments then landing to bob up and down like little paper boats on a pond.

Frantic sanderlings made punctured patterns on the sandy ridges, rushing hither and thither seemingly without purpose

whilst the stolid turnstones got on with the job of grubbing for sand - hoppers.
The oystercatchers, wading in the surf tried to call them to order with his sharp pill-pill but even his striking black and white plumage and orange beak could not distract them.

Certainly there was no shortage of food as the empty shells around testified.
Black mussel shells with pearly linings lay side by side with delicate pink tellins. Sharp edged razors, fan scallops and blue-tinged nutshells were empty houses; debris in the glistening tangle of bladder wrack by the water's edge.

Higher up the beach where the dunes began, low prickly Saltwort was interspersed with the pink and gold of Herb Robert and Knapweed.
Scarlet Pimpernel winked his eye cheerfully but the handsome black and yellow cinnabar caterpillars chewed unheeding as if conscious that only their diligent feeding could control the rampant ragwort.

I turned for a last glance, to see a skein of knots pulling the dusk like a final curtain across the horizon, folding the day softly into night.

****

Why do people order double cheeseburgers, large fries, and a diet coke?

Afternoon Tea

Richard Seal

"There are few hours in life more agreeable than the hour dedicated to the ceremony known as afternoon tea." - Henry James, The Portrait of a Lady

The taking of afternoon tea may well be regarded as one of the most typical of English customs. While the practice started thousands of years ago in China, and was popularised in the seventeenth century by King Charles II and his wife Catherine de Braganza, it was not until the mid nineteenth century that the concept of 'afternoon tea' first appeared in England. The drink's consumption increased dramatically around this time.

In 1840, Anna, the seventh Duchess of Bedford, found herself getting hungry at around four o'clock. Dinner in her household was not served until eight, a typical practice at that time, a long time since the last meal. The lady would ask that a tray of tea, bread and butter and cake be brought to her room during the late afternoon. This soon became a habit and she began inviting friends to join her,

By the 1880s the practice had become a fashionable social event - upper-class women would change into gowns, gloves and hats for tea which was served in the drawing room between four and five o'clock. While the upper classes would serve a 'low' or 'afternoon' tea, those of lower status had a more substantial 'high' tea later in the day instead of dinner. The names derive from the height of the tables used, high tea being at the dinner table.

Traditional afternoon tea consists of a selection of small sandwiches, and scones served with clotted cream and jam. Cakes and pastries are also provided. The drink is poured from silver tea pots into china cups. To experience the practice at its best, you may like to join the tourists and treat yourself to a trip to one of London's finest hotels or visit one of the many quaint English tearooms which can be found throughout the country.

****

Why is the man who invests all your money called a broker?

Foster Cat

Eighteen months after beloved tabby
had passed, the couple had started
feeling their way, slowly, tentatively,
towards considering a new addition
to the family. The tiny tortoiseshell,
a skinny, nervous, shadow sketch,
was considered awhile a foster cat
until, little by little, her bony angles
were softened, she filled out as fur
turned from coarse to velvet sheen.
Now no sharp bits remain as baby
snuggles tight purring deep in laps.

Richard Seal

Stories

Often found himself wallowing
in cosy-rosy nostalgia - settled
back in his armchair to savour
and share all the familiar tales,
anecdotes so well- rehearsed ..
But today, at last, a joyful first -
With grandson suddenly finds
in laughter a present moment
vivid in its glory - glad to play
a part in this unfolding story.

Richard Seal

Peace

Cathy loved staring out
of a window at nothing
in particular, always lost
in inner calm away from
outside world's potential
for much harm and alarm.
Happy to be written off
as an eccentric, content
to keep hold of her piece
of peace, joyous release.

Richard Seal

Ascent

Steve could not settle, refused
to stay put - always choosing
to be on the move, to improve
his experience of life, remove
all ties, connections, travelling
light without children or wife.
One day he stopped - remained
at the last place he went: never
seen again since a final attempt
at tackling mountain's ascent.

Richard Seal

Lawrence of Arabia

By Richard Seal

"By day the hot sun fermented us; and we were dizzied by the beating wind. At night we were stained by dew, and shamed into pettiness by the innumerable silences of stars." - T.E. Lawrence, Seven Pillars of Wisdom: A Triumph

Thomas Edward Lawrence (1888 - 1935), better known as Lawrence of Arabia, was a British archaeological scholar, military strategist, and author best known for his legendary war activities in the Middle East during World War I and for his account in 'The Seven Pillars of Wisdom'. Thomas was born in August 1888, in Caernarvonshire, Wales. The family settled in Oxford in 1896, and he went on to Jesus College. Medieval military architecture was his first interest.

Lawrence became an expert in Arab affairs as a junior archaeologist in Carchemish on the Euphrates River from 1911 to 1914, working on archaeological excavations. Travelling alone, he got to know the language and the people. Early in 1914 he explored northern Sinai, on the Turkish frontier east of Suez. Supposedly a scientific expedition, it was actually more a map-making observation from Gaza to Aqaba. The month the Great War began, Thomas became an employee of the Map Department of the

War Office, charged with preparing a military map of Sinai.

By December that year Lawrence was a lieutenant in Cairo. As an expert on Arab affairs, he was assigned to intelligence, where he spent over a year, interviewing prisoners, drawing maps, receiving data from agents behind enemy lines, and producing a handbook on the Turkish Army. In October 1916 he accompanied diplomat Sir Ronald Storrs on a mission to Arabia, where Ḥusayn ibn ʿAlī, amīr of Mecca, had the previous June proclaimed a revolt against the Turks. Back in Cairo in November, Thomas urged his superiors to aid efforts at rebellion.

Thomas joined Amir Faisal al Husayn's revolt against the Turks. He acted as political liaison officer, and led a guerrilla campaign. After a major victory at Aqaba, his forces supported British General Allenby's campaign to capture Jerusalem. In 1917, Lawrence was captured at Dar'a and tortured and abused, leaving permanent emotional scars. By the time the Arab army reached Damascus in October the following year, he was exhausted after having been wounded numerous times, captured, and tortured; he had also endured extremities of hunger, weather, and disease. By 1918, Lawrence had been promoted to lieutenant colonel and was awarded the Distinguished Service Order and the Order of Bath by

King George V. However, he refused both medals in support of Arab independence. His epic autobiographical book, 'The Seven Pillars of Wisdom' became known for its vivid descriptions of his many, varied campaigns in Arabia. The work brought Thomas international fame, and he was dubbed "Lawrence of Arabia." After the war, he joined the Royal Air Force under an assumed name, T.E. Shaw. He died in a motorcycle accident in May 1935, in Dorset, England.

Even before his most famous book was published in 1926, Lawrence had become a mythic figure in his own lifetime. More than just a military leader and inspirational force behind the Arab revolt against the Turks, he was also an excellent tactician and influential theoretician of guerrilla warfare. He created a characterisation rivaling any in contemporary fiction. A major film based on his life, 'Lawrence of Arabia', directed by David Lean and starring Peter O'Toole, was released in 1962. It went on to win seven Academy Awards, including the Oscar for best picture.

"All men dream: but not equally. Those who dream by night in the dusty recesses of their minds wake up in the day to find it was vanity, but the dreamers of the day are dangerous men, for they may act their dreams with open eyes, to make it possible." - T.E. Lawrence, Seven Pillars of Wisdom: A Triumph

My doctor said now that I'm older
I need to install a bar in the shower

Play

By Richard Seal

Arthur still feels disorientated after having been retired for six months. He is already tired of sitting at home watching daytime television, and pottering around in the garden. However, the man's spirits were lifted, and he felt a surge of inspiration when he saw a piece in the local paper about an amateur dramatics group who were looking for new members. As he stands in the car park outside the village hall, clutching the newspaper clipping, he can hear voices coming from inside the building.

The butterflies fluttering in the pit of his stomach take Arthur back half a century to the blood-chilling thrill of being in the play at High School: taking the part of the leading lady at a boys' grammar school, squeezed into his mother's tight dress, learning lines which have never been forgotten. The adrenalin rush was incredible, his family and friends were amazed and even the teachers seemed impressed. However, the exhilaration and elation had dissipated quickly when the final curtain fell.

Twenty years later Arthur tried his hand at acting again. He joined a theatre group who took themselves very seriously, and spent most of his time standing offstage, watching the protagonists strut their stuff. Before long he found himself reflecting on the futility of his unfulfilling struggle as prompt or understudy, never regarded as being quite ready for more than the smallest of parts, cameos lacking any dialogue.

Without energy or confidence, he waited in the wings for a while before losing heart and drifting away.

He hovers at the entrance to the building, wondering whether this bunch might be friendly and welcoming, acting for fun, or they could ask with disdain if he is capable of making the tea or shifting some scenery. Arthur does not feel up to being rejected or patronised. He turns away and starts to walk back to his car, wondering if he might be better suited to being in the audience rather than the cast. Suddenly the man stops, turns on his heels, and strides back towards the building, seized with fresh, grim resolve to be the Widow Twankey or die trying.

****

Rose Hip

By Richard Seal

Charlotte lived for her writing. She wielded wild words of joy, thrusting florid stanzas of love and lust at her rarified writers group over home-made cake and cups of rose hip tea. Her poems were lyrical touchstones, guaranteed to stir the heart, stimulate minds, fire the imagination. The woman's verse seemed like personal therapy, with streams of consciousness, emotions spilling into language, tears dropping through imagery down the page. Her first novel, a work in progress of many years' standing, packaged her muse into a tragic drama - Charlotte's voice was starting to be heard, shot through every word.

She had never arrived on time to the weekly writing group meetings, always seeming to be running late, on the verge of some kind of crisis, or needing to leave early. She would enter with a flourish looking fraught, then follow up with a theatrical disrobing of her flowing coat, pastel jacket and silk scarf. Charlotte had confided to one of the ladies, Jasmine, that she had been having some issues with alcohol lately, and had been seeing a counsellor on and off for a while. However, she usually preferred to keep her personal life concealed deep beneath chapters, blank verse, iambic pentameters. No one knew anything about her family, friends or relationships.

After attending the meeting one Wednesday evening in December, Charlotte had been driving home alone in strong winds and heavy rain down a country lane when her car had left the road and been involved in a head-on collision with a tree. She was killed instantly. No one witnessed what had happened at the sodden scene during that final mad dash and gruesome car crash. However, various members of the group came to the conclusion that, given that Charlotte's life had always been so disorganised and hectic, she could have been driving too fast in a reckless rush to get somewhere and had lost control at one of the tight bends. Or perhaps she had swerved violently to avoid striking an animal.

A few eyebrows were raised when it was revealed that Charlotte had left instructions for her own funeral. Some of the ladies speculated in whispers that she could even have orchestrated her dramatic demise. Jasmine wondered if she had been aware that her life would be cut so short, caught in full flight with no chance of any reprieve or retort. Or perhaps it had something to do with her drinking. The group, who had initially been shocked by their newest member, then regarded her with a degree of awe, claimed after her death that she had been much adored. This version of the story lasted for a few months, before people drifted, new ones joined, the memories began to fade, and were eventually ignored. The young writer's sudden death had struck a chord for a while with the bored of Chandler's Ford.

Stonehenge

By Richard Seal

"... Stonehenge really was the most incredible accomplishment. It took five hundred men just to pull each sarsen, plus a hundred more to dash around positioning the rollers. Just think about it for a minute. Can you imagine trying to talk six hundred people into helping you drag a fifty-ton stone eighteen miles across the countryside and muscle it into an upright position, and then saying, 'Right, lads! Another twenty like that, plus some lintels and maybe a couple of dozen nice bluestones from Wales, and we can party!' Whoever was the person behind Stonehenge was one dickens of a motivator, I'll tell you that." - Bill Bryson, Notes from a Small Island

For centuries, historians and archaeologists have discussed the many mysteries of Stonehenge, the prehistoric monument that took Neolithic builders an estimated one thousand five hundred years to erect. Located in Wiltshire in southern England, it comprises around a hundred massive upright stones placed in a circular layout. Whilst most scholars now agree that Stonehenge was once a burial ground, they have yet to determine what other purposes it served and how a civilisation without modern technology was able to build it. The construction is all the more intriguing because, while the sandstone slabs of its outer ring hail from local quarries, scientists have traced the bluestones that make up its inner ring all the way to the Preseli Hills in Wales.

Archaeologists believe that the iconic prehistoric ruin was

built in several stages, starting five thousand years ago. First, Neolithic Britons used primitive tools to dig a massive circular ditch and bank, or henge, on Salisbury Plain. Deep pits inside the circle dating back to that era may have once held a ring of timber posts. Several hundred years later, the builders hoisted around eighty bluestones, forty three of which remain today, into standing positions and placed them in either a horseshoe or circular formation. During the third phase of construction, in around 2000 B.C., sarsen sandstone slabs were arranged into an outer ring; some were assembled into the three-pieced trilithons that stand in the centre. Fifty of these stones are now visible on the site.

It seems likely that the monument's sarsen stones were sourced from quarries north of the site and transported using sledges and ropes. However, the smaller bluestones have been traced to the Preseli Hills in Wales, two hundred miles away. According to one theory, the builders made sledges and rollers out of trees to transport the stones. They were then transferred onto rafts and floated them along the Welsh coast and then up the Avon toward Salisbury Plain; alternatively, they may have towed each stone with a fleet of vessels. Others theorise that huge wicker baskets were used or a combination of ball bearings, long grooved planks and teams of oxen.

Early hypotheses attributed the monument's construction to the Saxons, Danes, Romans, Greeks or Egyptians. In the seventeenth century, archaeologist John Aubrey claimed that Stonehenge was the work of the Celtic high priests

known as the Druids, a theory widely popularized by William Stukeley, who had unearthed primitive graves at the site. Even today, modern Druids continue to gather at Stonehenge for the summer solstice. However, in the mid-twentieth century, radiocarbon dating demonstrated that the stones had stood for more than a millennia before the Celts inhabited the region.

Many modern historians and archaeologists now agree that several distinct groups of people contributed to the project, each undertaking a different phase of its construction. Bones, tools and other artifacts found on the site seem to support this idea. The first stage was achieved by Neolithic people who were indigenous to the British Isles. Later, it is believed, groups with advanced tools played their part in the development of the site. Some have suggested that they were European immigrants, but many scientists think that it is more likely that they were native Britons descended from the original builders.

The purpose of Stonehenge is even more of a mystery. There is strong archaeological evidence that it was used as a burial site, but most scholars believe it also served as a ceremonial site, a destination for religious pilgrimages, or a memorial to honour distant ancestors. In the 1960's, astronomer Gerald Hawkins suggested that the stones operated as an astronomical calendar, with different points corresponding to solstices, equinoxes and eclipses. While his theory has received some support, critics doubt that the builders possessed the knowledge necessary to predict such events. More recently, signs of illness and injury in human

remains unearthed at the site led a group of British archaeologists to speculate that it was considered a place of healing.
When Stonehenge was first opened to the public it was possible to walk among and even climb on the stones, but they have been roped off since 1977 as a result of serious erosion. Visitors are no longer permitted to touch them, but are able to walk around the monument from a short distance away. English Heritage does, however, permit access during the summer and winter solstice, and the spring and autumn equinox. Additionally, visitors can make special bookings to access the stones throughout the year.

One of the most famous and recognisable sites in the world, Stonehenge draws more than eight hundred thousand tourists a year. In 1986 it was added to UNESCO's register of World Heritage sites. The monument has undergone several restorations over the years, and some of its stones have been set in concrete to prevent collapse. Meanwhile, archaeological excavations and development of the surrounding area have turned up other significant sites nearby, including other 'henges'.

"There is something in Stonehenge almost reassuring; and if you are disposed to feel that life is rather a superficial matter, and that we soon get to the bottom of things, the immemorial gray pillars may serve to remind you of the enormous background of time." - Henry James

****

New Wife Needed

A young married man went to the Minister and told him he wanted to get married again.

The Minister said you can only have one wife.

The man looked dumb founded he said last time you said I could have four better, four worse, four richer, four poorer...that is sixteen.

****

The Short Straw

Trudie Oakley

Bob looked down at his paunch and sighed. How did he get to be a middle aged slightly overweight man with a receding hairline? He sat in his car watching all the young mums gathering at the school gate wondering how his life had been hijacked. He thought back to the day he'd married Beryl; they had been so happy – so full of vigour and ambition – they'd had their whole lives ahead of them but something somewhere had ground them down and now here he was just another older dad doing the school run.

He still loved Beryl but all the zing had gone out of their marriage. Most of the time their mutual affection for each other was demonstrated with a perfunctory kiss as they both left the house for work. They didn't make love any more, just had mechanical sex when they both had an itch. He wasn't

exactly unhappy but he was disappointed at the way things had turned out.
He remembered the excitement and pride he had felt when he had carried Beryl over the threshold of their first house. She had been heavily pregnant with twins then and life had been so full of promise. They moved into their semi a few years later and that is where they'd stayed. It was supposed to have been another stepping stone toward their dream house but practicalities like paying bills and family responsibilities got in the way and were increased somewhat when seven years later, and completely out of the blue, Beryl found that she was expecting another set of twins, so here they were still languishing in a sort of limbo – all dreams deferred, probably forever.
The school gates opened and children poured out onto the pavement reminding Bob of the hoards of scarab beetles he had seen running amuck in some silly film about Egyptian mummies coming back from the dead. He heaved himself out of the car ready to catch the twins' attention.
"Well blow me down! Its Bob isn't it? How the devil are you?"
Bob turned to put a face to the voice and found himself looking down at a thin deathly pale man sitting in a wheelchair who, despite the mild weather, was wearing a woolly hat and fleecy jacket and was largely covered by a blanket. He stared at the man completely at a loss – trying desperately to recognise this person who obviously knew him.
"I'm sorry but ..."

The man laughed and pulled off his hat revealing a bald head. "If I had any hair you'd remember me. It's Tony, Tony Morrison – from Hastings Tech."
"Ginger? Ginger Morrison – I'm so sorry mate I just didn't..."
"Course you didn't. Sorry to catch you out like that but I just had to speak to you – for old times' like."
"But what; I mean." Bob was embarrassed, and being lost for words just gestured toward the chair.
"Just bad luck I'm afraid. It's a long story mate but it seems that I'm nearly at the end of the road now; doctors reckon I might have three or four months left." Ginger replaced his hat smiling, "Ironic isn't it, I know we had some wild times for a while there, but I've never smoked, never been a real drinker," he pursed his lips, "actually I've lived quite a sober life ever since I got married, but there you are – I drew the short straw didn't I mate."
Before Bob could think of anything to say James and Sarah appeared and unsure of what to do or say, stood quietly on either side of their father.
Realising there wasn't much more to be said under the circumstances Ginger held out a hand. "I've got to go now but it's great to see you looking so well Bob," he looked at the twins "Did you marry that girl – what was her name now?"
"Beryl; yes it's our twenty fifth next year," he tried to make light of the situation "Some would say I'm a glutton for punishment."
Ginger leant forward and took his hand "Remember me to Beryl – she was a bit of alright she was - and have a good life mate."

Bob stood holding onto his children as he watched Ginger's wheelchair disappear into the busy throng. He had such fond memories of those days when he and Ginger were apprenticed electricians. Everyone knew Ginger – mad as a March Hare and always up to some prank or another. He'd nearly got them both thrown off their course on more than one occasion. He had been so full of joie de vivre - so vital, and now some cruel twist of fate was going to stamp out his life as though he was no more than some old unwanted weed.
"Who was that old man dad? Was he lost?"
"No, but maybe I was."
Sensing Bob's mood the twins sat quietly in the back of the car as their father taxied them home. He pulled into the drive and wondered why he had not noticed how pretty the garden looked. It was neat as a new pin and beautiful sweetly perfumed hanging baskets adorned the house. From the kitchen Bob watched the family washing blowing gently in the breeze, Beryl must have done that before she started her shift. He had been blinded by complacency; she did so much for all of them and over the years he had taken her more and more for granted. He felt suddenly humble – how on earth could he have questioned their life together. They had four beautiful children, a beautiful home and the rest of their lives to enjoy it all – he was one of the luckiest men on the planet.
The kettle had just come to the boil when Beryl bustled in. "I'm afraid it will have to be sausages tonight folks – I forgot to get any meat out of the freezer so ...."
Bob slid his arms around his slightly startled wife. "Tonight my dear we are getting a take-away. We'll wait until Isla and

John get home from college then we can make a democratic decision as to what we get." James and Sarah immediately started jumping up and down, one calling out for Indian, the other Chinese. They ran off to watch television still arguing the point.

Bob sat at the kitchen table across from his wife and they sat sipping tea in the contented silence that only comes when two people are truly comfortable with each other. Bob was just about to mention his encounter with Ginger when he heard the hinge creak on the front gate – he made a mental note to make sure he oiled it and to catch up on the many small jobs that he had neglected of late.

He called out to the twins "Quick you two, John and Isla are home – turn off the telly and let's surprise them."

Bob grabbed Beryl's hand and along with the two giggling excited youngsters they squeezed into the cupboard under the stairs.

Beryl had been a little worried about their marriage lately and had begun to wonder if Bob really loved her any more, but tonight he was more like his old mischievous self. She couldn't help wondering what had brought about the change in her husband but was more than happy to crouch in that dark stuffy cupboard – it had been a long time since they'd had any fun.

****

Why is it that doctors and attorneys call what they do 'practice'?

The Battle of the Somme

On the anniversary of the first day of The Battle of the Somme

- A poem for Remembrance Day
By Ellie Jenkins

It was 1916 on the 1st of July
That artillery and smoke blackened the sky.
Shots rang out and men fell dead,
The sky was black, while the ground was red.
To battle the Germans the French and British had come,
To the bloodiest fight of the War, The Battle of the Somme.
While artillery rained down on the German side
The allies swallowed their fear and stood with pride.
Waiting to be ordered over the top,
To run without question, don't look back and don't stop.
But this is when the slaughter started,
Machine guns screamed out as bodies and limbs became parted.
Fifty-eight thousand casualties in one single day
'A necessary loss' the Generals would say.
'We will rest for now and recommence tomorrow
No time for the men to indulge in their sorrow'
So they readied the next batch of men for the slaughter,

Story Telling Twelve

Would they fare better when faced with the mortars?
The answer to this question was obviously no
As the casualty counts continued to grow.
For every single centimeter of ground that was taken
The lives of two men were sadly forsaken.
And so the battle waged on and on,
The bloodiest battle of World War One.
Yet as they made progress towards German lines,
The Allies had one thing in the front of their minds.
For the Germans had a weapon the Allies had yet to discover
One that would find men even if they took cover.
As the allied assault drew nearer and nearer
The time to use this weapon had never been clearer.
The little grey canisters flew through the air
Giving the allied forces more than a scare.
The men now engaged in a fight for their lives,
They could not protect themselves with their guns or their knives.
Their only weapon now was a mask
But fitting it in time was a very hard task.
'Gas, Gas!' some men would cry
Most had masks, the rest would die.

Story Telling Twelve

Their screams could be heard as they approached their death,
Blood curdled in their lungs as they drew their last breath.
Eventually their eyes would roll back in their head
And with a final twitch and spasm they lay still, dead.
And so the battle waged on and on,
The bloodiest battle of World War One.
Even with the threat of the German gas,
It was time for a final allied assault to mass.
And with this Britain unveiled their tank
When the battle ended they had this to thank.
It stormed over No-Man's Land, through German wire,
The Germans shook in fear as it prepared to fire.
For the British troops it opened the way,
For the deaths of their comrades the Germans would pay.
And the German death count grew and grew
As the allied assault continued to break through.
And though the fighting had not ended,
The morale of the Allies began to get mended.
They pushed with valor towards their objective,
With a new vigor the Germans had not expected.
Although the enemy held, and did not retreat
This battle is viewed as a German defeat.

Story Telling Twelve

It was 1916 on the 21st of November
That the five month long battle was finally over.
No shots rang out but thousands were dead,
The sky was still black, the ground was stained red.
To battle the Germans the French and British had come,
To the bloodiest fight of the War, The Battle of the Somme.

****

You know that indestructible black box that is used on airplanes? Why don't they make the whole plane out of that stuff??

Somewhere in Paris

The foreword from Percy's thrilling Novel 'Politically Incorrect'

Just prior to the large increase in oil prices in 1974, an influential Arab, who had the ability to soften the blow for the industrial nations, sat at the head of the table in the boardroom of one of his many companies. His patience was wearing thin as the monthly meeting stretched beyond its time limit.

Outside the heavy curtained window that overlooked a narrow Paris street leading to the Champs Elysees, the sun was vying with the clouds in an attempt to warm the city. At the end of the turning, seated beneath a coloured awning amongst numerous tables and chairs, Paulo looked at his watch and noted that their schedule was starting to run late.

He looked down the street. Half-way along his companion waited in a Transit van, which had been acquired for the occasion. The bonnet was open, on the pretence that it had broken down. Sue, a pretty and yet nondescript-looking girl, was patiently waiting behind the wheel. Passersby and traffic police glanced at the stricken vehicle and without further thought continued about their business.

Paulo looked at his watch once more and pondered on the wisdom of ordering a third cup of coffee. His prey was nearly an hour late from the timings of his normal monthly meeting, and the agreed time limit between the partners had expired. He continued to wait, years of experience guiding him. At his feet a duffel bag concealed an automatic small arms weapon loaded and cocked, waiting to spit out its deadly missiles at the hands of the master who temporarily possessed it.

Beyond the van, patiently waiting in front of a tall office block in a small slip road, stood a limousine. Its owner a few floors up looked at the wall clock, and with firmness, as he came to a decision he stood up, declaring the meeting closed, adding that the matter being discussed was wasting his time, and could be put on the agenda for the next monthly meeting. Immaculately dressed in a dark business suit, he left the room.

Had anybody been observing that meeting, they would have noticed that there was one who had been trying to hurry matters along, knowing that time was short if the plan that had been devised to destroy the powerful objection to their course was to take place. Hastily looking at his watch as the meeting broke up, he hoped that the paid assassins had waited longer than arranged.

The light grey Mercedes edged away from the building into the street and slowly made its way towards Paris's main thoroughfare less than two hundred metres from where it had waited. Nobody noticed that the bonnet of the van was closed and that the engine sprang into life as Sue regained the driving seat.

Discarding his third cup of coffee Paulo walked towards the junction with the famous street, his timing matching the pace of the big car.

The car and the gunman arrived at the junction at the same time. The Arab, busy studying papers in the rear, was not aware of his surroundings, only one of his two bodyguards taking any notice of Paulo, and then without any alarm. Sue pulled the van away from the kerb, following the larger car a short distance behind, the sliding side doors locked in the open position. The Mercedes stopped at the junction, and the driver looked in horror as the young person dropped the bag. In his hand the sterling sub machine gun looked black and ugly

The bodyguard, who had given the man but a cursory glance, suddenly realised the danger and loudly cursed his lack of alertness. He watched as the gun, which appeared to be moving in slow motion, swung round towards him. He swiftly went for his own revolver tucked in a holster under his arm, knowing that he would not make it.

His boss, sensing the danger, looked up, and as he did so he saw the flashes from the stubby barrel of the automatic as the weapon spat out its message. Pedestrians stopped and stared as the noise echoed around the busy streets and buildings. The windows of the car disintegrated, the blood sprayed its interior as the men died instantly. Only the chauffeur remained alive, severely wounded as he slumped over the wheel, setting the horn off in an incessant blast.

Paulo left the scene, knowing his mission was accomplished. Sprinting to the van that was gathering speed, he threw himself in through the open side door and disappeared, with Sue expertly steering the vehicle through the traffic. Minutes later, their disguises removed the van abandoned, the couple vanished.

From the novel 'Politically Incorrect by Percy Chattey

The Swarm:

By Christopher Wyatt

The setting: A house in Spain on a mountainside overlooking a small village with two old friends studying the valley and mulling over events with a glass of wine

Oxford Dictionary 1987 definitions
Swarm (swawm) n. 1 a large number of small animals, people etc., esp. when moving in a confused mass.

"The wine is good",
The two old friends were seated comfortably in the bower of 'The Heights' overlooking the valley and the village below.
"Indeed" said James, "It is from our own grapes, we were lucky that some of the vines survived"
"Well it is good indeed, no matter whose feet did the treading" Michael exclaimed, "I have always favoured the local wine myself". Indeed, his lips were stained red, an indication perhaps of the amount he had drunk.
James took a sip, set down his glass and gazed into the distance. He frowned, turned to Michael and said, "Do you hear that?"

Michael looked at him, "No" he replied shortly. James raised a sardonic eyebrow. Everyone knew that his friend was deaf. "Where?"
James looked across the bower and down the valley, "There, along the valley floor".
There was a pause while both men addressed their wine.
"There", said James again, "I can see dust".
"Oh yes, down to the left"
A faint haze seemed to be rising, slightly obscuring the lower road which led to the village.
"I can feel it too", Michael paused, "Have you your binoculars?"
"Yes, Jean, can you get my glasses please?"
Jean brought out the binoculars, James put it to his eye and peered down into the valley.
"There is a dark mass coming along the road, spilling out to either side".
"I CAN hear them now and, feel that tremor, let me see" Michael took the offered glasses, "By the Gods, it's a swarm!"
"A swarm?" said Jean,
"Yes, it's people, thousands of people. The dispossessed. The swarm. It moves forward constantly; boundaries are no deterrent. They cannot stop moving for to stop is to die. Like

locusts they devour everything in their path and leave desolation behind them"

"God knows you are right. I recall now, they started years ago as refugees moving from country to country looking for a place to settle. Driven on each time by the armies of those lands until they took on a life of their own".

"They have gone through the lands of the East and spread into the Western countries of Europus, even moving across the seas when the bodies of the drowned washed up on the shores around".

Michael looked thoughtful, "We should be safe up here, not in a direct line of the swarm, they could pass by for hours yet".

The front of the swarm was now clearly visible, a vast mass of people moving almost at a run and spreading out to either side of the road. Then the leaders hit the first of the village houses. There came a growl of sound, a low rumble that echoed up the valley. A cloud of dust rose up, obscuring the front onslaught of the swarm. "You either join and run with them or they will consume you along with everything in their path" exclaimed James.

The swarm moved on through the village, consuming and destroying as it went. On and on it rolled, relentless in its movement like a

wave, always flowing forward, never ebbing. The outriders were channelled through the side streets, taking - never stopping long enough to enjoy. The weight of the people coming on behind would not let them. Consume or die.
It was around four hours before the last stragglers came in sight. The old, the weak, the sick; gradually losing ground, passing through the swarm moving slower and slower until at last they were spat out at the end, staggering, gradually starving and dying. The path of the swarm was marked by the corpses of the fallen.
"By God", James looked upon the ruins of what had been a substantial village. The dust was gradually settling over the remains of houses, shops and the detritus of a swarm on the move. The stench of their passing had not yet reached the friends and as they gazed on the devastation below, more wine was called for and drunk to try and blot out their memories.
"Volunteers for burial squad" came the call.

Dictionary Amendment (Year 5 New Era)
Swarm; The. A mass of people unstopping, forever moving forward. A destructive force. First noticed during the movement of refugees across the Continent during the 2000's.

Burial party. An opportunity to get extra rations and a seat, (more importantly a voice), on the Council. The two friends trudged down to the village and joined the team around the local fore-man.

They collected their spades and walked along in silence to the farthest village boundary, about a klick from the centre, in order to start work. There was not much disturbance to be seen this far out, bushes and small trees flattened after being stripped of all useful nourishment. People had learned to keep anything of value buried as the swarm never stayed long enough to dig, only to destroy.

The bodies were the usual mix of the very old, the very young and those crippled by the continual movement.

“Hope they get the wagon down here more quickly this time, the heat won’t do these much good”

“No, anything worth recycling on your side?” Michael looked around at bodies scattered along the trail.

“No” said James, “Everything worn to rags.” The first thing you noticed was, no shoes. Then a lack of clothing, rags mostly, perhaps less than that on some of them, just a cloth and string to preserve whatever modesty they had left or

perhaps just to keep the delicate areas covered from the dust and heat.
The younger ones had even less. But no-one lusted after young flesh any more. Worn down by lack of food and the constant movement, these were the remnants, the dross and rubbish left behind by the swarm. To be covered up as swiftly as possible before they rotted and contaminated what was left of civilisation!
'Civilisation', a word, a description of something that appeared to be rapidly disintegrating. We were 'Civilised'. We didn't eat our dead (yet) and we kept up the practices of our parents and their parents before them, that is to say, we did not kill each other unnecessarily! We ploughed the fields and scattered all right, we ploughed in the remains of the swarm and scattered their ground down bones as fertiliser!
Like them, we wasted nothing. We could not afford to. Waste was death. How had this happened? How did we fall so far from a society of countries and cities, towns, villages, a way of life that now seems so far gone that only the old, those that have survived that is, seem to remember?
Civilisation! A word. Civilised, be good to your neighbour. Respect others not only your own people, your own religion, your own sexual

orientation. So many facets of society to be 'civilised' to and now? Now can be summed up by 'Watch thy neighbour' and if he falters, be prepared to enter his home and strip it clean. Look after the poor widow for when she dies, you can be first to search for her hidden trove. That, my friends, is civilisation. Eat or be eaten. Not literally of course, we leave that particular barbarism to the swarm, just figuratively, by keeping an eye on the main subject, one's own survival.

I have survived, keeping my eyes on the main chance and plunging in to look after my own interests but I would like to think that I have not lost *all* my humanity. So I remember. I remember when this all began. My memories direct or those of others passed to me in tales? A bit of both I would say, who now could take fact from fiction anyway?

Back in the early 2000's (old reckoning), wars and conflict seemed to span the globe. Those that had refused to share with those that had not. Those at 'peace', turned away from those at war and so were sowed the seeds of our destruction.

In those glory days (to us at any rate) we spanned the continent of Europe. My wife and I, travelling like so many others, from Holland through Germany and on to those Eastern countries which had laboured so long under the religion of 'Communism'. I think it would have been around 2015 or '16 that the world first started noticing a movement of large numbers of people across Europe. I can remember seeing pictures of long columns of the 'dispossessed' (as they were called then) stretching through the Eastern European countryside. There appeared to be no goal save for that of reaching a country that would take them in, feed and clothe them and give them work. Yet there appeared that no country, (except Germany originally) was willing to accept not just the hundreds of thousands of the now, but the uncounted millions poised to march later.

Little did we know, or should I say rather that our leaders knew, just how devastating would be the result of slamming the doors. One country after another sealed its borders, in the East of Europe, the old ways came to the fore with barbed wire and machine guns. We shall never know how many died then, thousands of men, women and children bulldozed into great pits and buried. But it didn't stop the movement of people. After a while it appeared that nothing would. Even the most brutal amongst us tires of *killing and shamefacedly shoulders his weapon, marching away to his home town or village.*

The fences eroded, the guards (except for the most obstinate) had gone, the way was open and the swarm started to take shape. The movement of large numbers of the dispossessed moved across the land, swallowing up what had been left. Then the different streams of people started to split because where one had passed, there was nothing for the next wave to take up and use. There came the need to move faster, to get the possessions of what was left before the next wave and so was born The Swarm. Ever moving, never stopping to rest. To stop was to starve and die. Movement was all and you faltered at your peril. And so we fell. We? Yes, we the 'civilised'. We, the ones who were static. Who remained where we were placed, 'home', that's where we stayed. To protect what was ours, to survive, to live as best we could while the Swarm moved through the country, the Continent, the World, never stopping, never ceasing to destroy in order to live. Was their motivation any different to ours? I don't know but not much I would say. All we do now is grow our crops, bury our goods and pray to whichever Gods we happen to worship that the Swarm passes us by.

Red Squirrels
Drive slowly

Why are they allowed to drive?

****

If flying is so safe, why do they call the airport the terminal?

Why are they called apartments when they are all stuck together?

A FAMILY SECRET

By Carole Llewellyn

It was time for the truth. Twenty years of silence, of hurting, of pretending. She had been sixteen, unmarried and pregnant. To avoid a scandal her strict parents adopted the baby. Overnight her son became her brother. She hoped for forgiveness.

The door opened. 'Hello, sis,' he said. 'Hello, *son*,' she replied.

Questions, answers and hopefully, forgiveness…?

****

Why do supermarkets make the sick walk all the way to the back of the store to get their prescriptions while healthy people can buy cigarettes at the front

CLOCKS

Lin Penhaul

I feel as if I´m in a time warp.

The round faced clock high on the kitchen wall says twenty past three and I know it can´t be twenty past three because the last time I looked it said seven thirty and I´m sure that was only a few minutes ago when I came in to make breakfast.

I walk into the dining room where the gold carriage clock on the unit still says exactly eight thirty which is where it stopped a week ago and refused all efforts to start it . I think it needs cleaning again.

In the first bedroom the travel alarm clock on the bedside cabinet lies miserably on its back staring at the ceiling, one hand missing.

The second bedroom has two clocks, a watch and a mobile phone. Surely one of them will give me the correct time?

As I reach for the bedside clock it slips from my eager grasp and skitters under the bed to join the dust bunnies in the furthest corner of the room.

Story Telling Twelve

The pretty little green and red wall clock has a habit of slowing down every few hours and then rushing along to try and catch up with itself but unless you know which phase it´s going through it´s totally useless.

My solar powered wristwatch has been shut in the box too long and needs a boost from the sun to get it started again.

Scrabbling in the drawer for my mobile phone I switch it on only to be faced with a blank screen indicating an exhausted battery.

My last hope is the television set in the living room.
Why didn´t I think of this first, I wonder?

When I switch on I am immediately faced with a weather forecaster predicting snow, ice, freezing fog and high winds.

Without stopping to look at the time I rush back into my bed and dive under the covers.

****

An answer I can understand....
An American tourist asks an Irishman: "Why do Scuba divers always fall backwards off their boats?"
To which the Irishman replies: "If they fell forwards, they'd still be in the bloody boat."

WHY DOGS LIVE LESS THAN HUMAN

Here's the surprising answer of a 6 year old child.

Being a veterinarian, I had been called to examine a ten-year-old Irish Wolfhound named Belker. The dog's owners, Ron, his wife Lisa, and their little boy Shane, were all very attached to Belker, and they were hoping for a miracle.

I examined Belker and found he was dying of cancer. I told the family we couldn't do anything for Belker, and offered to perform the euthanasia procedure for the old dog in their home.

As we made arrangements, Ron and Lisa told me they thought it would be good for six-year-old Shane to observe the procedure. They felt as though Shane might learn something from the experience.

The next day, I felt the familiar catch in my throat as Belker's family surrounded him. Shane seemed so calm, petting the old dog for the last time, that I wondered if he understood what was going on. Within a few minutes, Belker slipped peacefully away.

The little boy seemed to accept Belker's transition without any difficulty or confusion. We sat together for a while after Belker's Death, wondering aloud about the sad fact that dogs' lives are shorter than human lives. Shane, who had been listening quietly, piped up, "I know why."

Startled, we all turned to him. What came out of his mouth next stunned me. I'd never heard a more comforting explanation. It has changed the way I try and live.

He said, "People are born so that they can learn how to live a good life — like loving everybody all the time and being nice, right?" The six-year-old continued,

"Well, dogs already know how to do that, so they don't have to stay for as long as we do."

Live simply.
Love generously.
Care deeply.
Speak kindly.

Remember, if a dog was the teacher you would learn things like:

• When your loved ones come home, always run to greet them.
• Never pass up the opportunity to go for a joyride.
• Allow the experience of fresh air and the wind in your face to be pure Ecstasy.
• Take naps.
• Stretch before rising.
• Run, romp, and play daily.
• Thrive on attention and let people touch you.
• Avoid biting when a simple growl will do.

• On warm days, stop to lie on your back on the grass.
• On hot days, drink lots of water and lie under a shady tree.
• When you're happy, dance around and wag your entire body.
• Delight in the simple joy of a long walk.
• Be faithful.
• Never pretend to be something you're not.
• If what you want lies buried, dig until you find it.
• When someone is having a bad day, be silent, sit close by, and nuzzle them gently.

That's the secret of happiness that we can learn from a good dog.

Adventurer

Danny never minds waiting around at airports, being unsure about his gate, facing long queues and much confusion. He has long since reached the conclusion that such things are part of the fun en route to reaching exotic places: exciting, edgy, perhaps a little odd, strangely, vaguely fragrant in the sun. Finding his plane delayed for several hours, Danny settles back into a seat, sips a coffee and looks around, oblivious to the sound of busy, complaining chitter chatter - An undisturbed calm within despite the clatter crashing din.

Focusing on his breath, content to be present and still, Danny is actively aware without a thought or intent. He sees a family speed by, huge suitcases threatening to buckle their tiny wheels, a bleary-eyed stag party wavering along, a heavily bearded student wearing headphones and a profound frown, and a couple barely speaking, heavily absorbed in their smart phones. He feels calmness in sense perceptions, having moved beyond mental constructs into a space somewhere in between: joy and peace in the now. He feels so relieved to be in a place he knows he will never leave.

A cramped seat, babies crying, and even a drunk man sitting beside him on the flight cannot bring Danny down; the only thing which could cause this adventurer to frown would be turning the plane around. Every year Danny takes himself off to Benidorm for a mini break alone. He smiles seeing tourists stumbling between bars or sleeping off hangovers on the beach, having done such things so often himself, a lifetime ago. The special cafe in a quiet side street where he met his beloved wife was closed down shortly after she passed away. As he turns eighty over tapas, sitting amongst locals in a tavern, the waiter's smile as he pours the wine leaves Danny so happy to be in this moment

****

SENIOR DRIVING

As a senior citizen was driving down the freeway, his car phone rang. Answering, he heard his wife's voice urgently warning him, 'Herman, I just heard on the news that there's a car going the wrong way on Interstate 77. Please be careful!' 'Heck,' said Herman, 'It's not just one car. It's hundreds of them!'

Peace

Cathy loved staring out
of a window at nothing
in particular, always lost
in inner calm away from
outside world's potential
for much harm and alarm.
Happy to be written off
as an eccentric, content
to keep hold of her piece
of peace, joyous release.

****

The Blitz

Percy Chattey

In the declining light of a September evening, at the countless German military airfields across Europe, the Luftwaffe prepared for the first of what would be scores of bombing raids of the Blitz against Britain. The noise of thousands of aerial engines extended across the land as they came to life. With one purpose in mind the giant planes, their wings spread out to each side gathered speed as they swept across the ground lifting themselves with their heavy loads into the sky.

Like a giant swarm of locusts they headed west into the fading sun making their way to the English Channel and the coastline of the Kent countryside. The Dormiers, Heinkals with others, spread out in line, protected by a horde of Messerschmitt fighter planes as they approached their targets, the docklands and industrial sites of East London. The RAF facilities in and around the rural area on the outskirts of the city.

Airfields across the land, Hornchurch, Epping, Biggin Hill amongst many more became a hive of activity as the famous few of fighter pilots raced to their Spitfires and Hurricanes to take off without delay climbing rapidly into the air to combat the raiders.

People stared at the sky in horror...listening to the noise like a constant rumble of thunder. They watched the bombers in a line, twenty seven miles wide with many more immediately behind as they crossed the coast in a flood. Others flew directly along the River Thames towards the industrial sites dotted along each side. With air raid warning screaming out their message people ran for cover to protect themselves against the onslaught.

In the Air Raid Shelter made of steel, two people were holding each other tightly, listening to the constant noise of the night raiders as they pounded the city with their bombs. They could also hear the gunfire from the local 'Ack Ack' station as they tried to repel the enemy bombers who were coming over in wave after wave.

Story Telling Twelve

There was a whistle as a bomb fell from the sky and then another a little nearer, followed by two more each one louder. The explosions that followed as they hit the ground rocked the shelter. The next in the line screeched as it hurtled downwards was more ear splitting than the others.

They prayed holding each other tightly knowing the last one was very near. Suddenly, the noise of the explosion drowned even their screams, the shelter shuddered, the concrete base splitting like a piece of paper as their steel cover was blown on to its side

WWW.PERCYCHATTEYBOOKS.COM
STORY TELLING
Unique & Different

www.ingramcontent.com/pod-product-compliance
Lightning Source LLC
Chambersburg PA
CBHW060521030426
42337CB00015B/1960

* 9 7 8 1 9 1 6 4 6 9 7 0 9 *